First World War
and Army of Occupation
War Diary
France, Belgium and Germany

1 INDIAN CAVALRY DIVISION
Divisional Troops
1 Brigade Royal Horse Artillery
2 September 1914 - 31 December 1916

WO95/1170/1

The Naval & Military Press Ltd
www.nmarchive.com
Published in association with The National Archives

Published by

The Naval & Military Press Ltd

Unit 10 Ridgewood Industrial Park,

Uckfield, East Sussex,

TN22 5QE England

Tel: +44 (0) 1825 749494

www.naval-military-press.com

www.nmarchive.com

This diary has been reprinted in facsimile from the original. Any imperfections are inevitably reproduced and the quality may fall short of modern type and cartographic standards.

© **Crown Copyright**
Images reproduced by permission of The National Archives, London, England, 2015.

Contents

Document type	Place/Title	Date From	Date To
Heading	WO95/1170/1		
Heading	BEF 1 Indian Cav. Div Troops Bde R.H.A 1914 Sett To 1916 Dec Design Ten 16 Bde R.H.A 1916 Dec To 4 Cav Dix Troops Box 1158		
Heading	War Diary of Head Quarters R.H.A. 1st Indian Cavalry Division. From 2nd September 1914 to 5th February 1915		
War Diary		02/09/1914	29/06/1915
Heading	War Diary of R.A. Head Quarters. 1st Indian Cavalry Division. From 1st February 1915 To 28th February 1915		
War Diary		31/01/1915	01/02/1915
War Diary	Ypres	06/02/1915	13/02/1915
War Diary	Norrent Fontes	13/02/1915	13/02/1915
War Diary	Ypres	01/02/1915	02/02/1915
War Diary	Following Daily N. Fonts Were.	02/02/1915	03/02/1915
War Diary	Ypres	04/02/1915	28/02/1915
Miscellaneous	Appendix I	29/01/1915	29/01/1915
Miscellaneous	Appendix II		
Heading	War Diary with Appendices of Head Quarters R.A. 1st Indian Cavalry Division. From 1st March 1915 To 31st March 1915		
War Diary	Norrent Fontes	01/03/1915	04/03/1915
War Diary	Lavantie	05/03/1915	06/03/1915
War Diary	Rue De Paradis-Laventie	06/03/1915	30/03/1915
Miscellaneous	Appendix II Instructions For Action 8th Division and attached Artillery	09/03/1915	09/03/1915
Miscellaneous	Appendix III		
Miscellaneous	1st Phase The Bombardment		
Miscellaneous	2nd Phase		
Miscellaneous	3rd Phase After Trench Is Taken		
Miscellaneous			
Miscellaneous	Appendix III		
Miscellaneous	Appendix 4 A		
Miscellaneous			
Miscellaneous	Appendix IV A.	10/03/1915	10/03/1915
Miscellaneous	A Form. Messages And Signals. Appendix IV B		
Miscellaneous	A Form. Messages And Signals.		
Miscellaneous	Appendix IV B Instructions For VII Division And Attached Artillery	11/03/1915	11/03/1915
Miscellaneous	Appendix IV B	11/03/1915	11/03/1915
Miscellaneous	A Form. Messages And Signals. Appendix V		
Miscellaneous	Appendix V		
Miscellaneous	A Form. Messages And Signals. Appendix 5 H		
Miscellaneous	Appendix VA		
Miscellaneous	Appendix V A		
Miscellaneous	Appendix V A	13/03/1915	13/03/1915
Miscellaneous	Instructions For VII Divisional and Attached Artillery For 12th March 1915 Appendix VI	12/03/1915	12/03/1915
Miscellaneous	A Form. Messages And Signals. Appendix VII		

Miscellaneous	14th Bd.		
Miscellaneous			
Miscellaneous	14 Clue with nearest Bn to them		
Miscellaneous	C Form (Duplicate). Messages And Signals Appendix VII		
Miscellaneous	C Form (Duplicate). Messages And Signals		
Miscellaneous	Appendix VII		
Miscellaneous	A Form. Messages And Signals. Appendix VIII		
Miscellaneous	A Form. Messages And Signals.		
Diagram etc			
Miscellaneous	Information on area between communication		
Miscellaneous	A Form. Messages And Signals.		
Miscellaneous	O.C. "A" "Q" "N"		
Miscellaneous	Special Order.	09/03/1915	09/03/1915
Map	Right Section 8th Division		
Map			
Heading	Div R.A		
Map	Centre Section 8th Division		
Map	Maps		
Map	Left Section 8th Division		
Map	Maps		
Heading	With Appendices War Diary of Head Quarters R.A 1st Indian Cavalry Division From 7th April 1915 To 28th May 1915		
War Diary	Rue De Paradis Laventie	07/04/1915	17/04/1915
War Diary	Fleurbaix	20/04/1915	21/04/1915
War Diary	La Croix Lescornex Fleurbaix	22/04/1915	01/05/1915
War Diary	Watau	02/05/1915	03/05/1915
War Diary	Fleurbaix	03/05/1915	10/05/1915
War Diary	Gorre	11/05/1915	11/05/1915
War Diary	Reference 1/10,000 Illies-Viollaines Festibert	12/05/1915	16/05/1915
War Diary	1/2 Miles W Of Festubert	16/05/1915	28/05/1915
Map	1st RHA Bde		
Miscellaneous	Copies of Telephone Messages.	05/05/1915	05/05/1915
Miscellaneous	Supply of Ammunition	05/05/1915	05/05/1915
Miscellaneous	1st H.A. Bde.	19/05/1915	19/05/1915
Miscellaneous	List of Enemy Gun Positional within 6,000 yards, which have been located by Airmen within the last ten days but it is not known which are and which are not occupied.		
Miscellaneous	1st Brigade R H A	20/05/1915	20/05/1915
Miscellaneous	1st Brigade R.H.A.	20/05/1915	20/05/1915
Heading	War Diary of 1st Indian R.H.A. Brigade. 1st Indian Cavalry Division June-December-1915		
Heading	War Diary of 1st Indian R.H.A Brigade Form 15th June 1915 To 30.th June 11915		
War Diary	Rubrouck	15/06/1915	30/06/1915
Heading	War Diary of 1st Indian R.H.A. Brigade. From 1st July 1915 To 31st July 1915		
War Diary	Quiestede	01/07/1915	01/07/1915
War Diary	Chateau La Preule	10/07/1915	12/07/1915
War Diary	Therouanne	29/07/1915	30/07/1915
Heading	War Diary of Head Quarters 1st Indian R.H.A. Brigade. From 1st August 1915 To 31st August 1915		
War Diary	Therouanne	01/08/1915	04/08/1915
War Diary	Lahaie Surcamp	07/08/1915	12/08/1915
War Diary	La Haie	23/08/1915	26/08/1915

Heading	War Diary of Head Quarter 1st Indian R.H.A. Brigade From 1st September 1915 To 30th September 1915		
War Diary	La Haie Surcamps	05/09/1915	22/09/1915
War Diary	Heuzecourt	24/09/1915	25/09/1915
Heading	War Diary of Head Quarters 1st Indian R.H.A. Brigade. From 1st October 1915 To 31st October 1915		
War Diary	Heuzecourt	01/10/1915	13/10/1915
War Diary	Vauchelles	15/10/1915	18/10/1915
War Diary	Soues	22/10/1915	27/10/1915
Heading	War Diary of 1st Indian R.H.A. Brigade From 1st November 1915 To 30th November 1915		
War Diary	Soues	04/11/1915	11/11/1915
War Diary	Croquoison	18/11/1915	23/11/1915
Heading	War Diary of 1st Indian R.H.A. Brigade. From 1st December 1915 To 31st December 1915		
War Diary	Croquoison	04/12/1915	16/12/1915
War Diary	Beauchamps	17/12/1915	31/12/1915
Heading	War Diary of Head Quarters 1st Indian R.H.Q. Brigade From 1st January 1916 To 31st January 1916		
War Diary	Beauchamps	01/01/1916	17/01/1916
Heading	War Diary of 1st Indian R.H.A. Brigade. From 1st February 1916 To 29th February 1916		
War Diary	Beauchamps	04/02/1916	14/02/1916
War Diary	Offeux	16/02/1916	29/02/1916
Heading	War Diary of 1st Indian R.H.A. Brigade Headquarters. From 1st March 1916 To 31st March 1916		
War Diary	Offeux	02/03/1916	25/03/1916
War Diary	Quoeux	27/03/1916	31/03/1916
Heading	War Diary of 1st Indian R.H.A. Brigade Headquarters. From 1st April 1916 To 30 April 1916		
War Diary	Quoeux	01/04/1916	30/04/1916
Heading	War Diary of 1st Indian Royal Horse Artillery Brigade. From 1st May 1916 To 31st May 1916		
War Diary	Millencourt	01/05/1916	07/05/1916
War Diary	Quoeux	08/05/1916	31/05/1916
Heading	War Diary of Hd Qrs, 1st Indian R.H.A. Brigade. from 1st June 1916 To 30th June 1916		
War Diary	Field	03/06/1916	30/06/1916
Heading	War Diary of Headquarters. 1st Indian R.H.A. Brigade From 1st July 1916 To 31st July 1916		
War Diary	Doullens	02/07/1916	02/07/1916
War Diary	Bouvoir Riviere	06/07/1916	10/07/1916
War Diary	Wavans	11/07/1916	30/07/1916
War Diary	Trois Maison Maroeuil	31/07/1916	31/07/1916
Heading	War Diary of Headquarters 1st Indian R.H.A Brigade. From 1st August 1916 To 31st August 1916		
War Diary	Maroeuil	01/08/1916	31/08/1916
Heading	War Diary of H. Qrs. 1st Indian Royal Horse Artillery Brigade. From 1st September 1916 To 30th September 1916		
Heading	War Diary of R.H.A. Bde. Hd Qrs From 1st Sept 1916 To 30 Sept 1916 Volume I		
War Diary	Maroeuil	01/09/1916	08/09/1916
War Diary	Rebreuve	08/09/1916	09/09/1916
War Diary	Bealcourt	09/09/1916	09/09/1916
War Diary	Doullens	09/09/1916	11/09/1916

War Diary	Frechencourt	13/09/1916	13/09/1916
War Diary	Allenville	14/09/1916	14/09/1916
War Diary	Ville sur Ancre	15/09/1916	25/09/1916
War Diary	Montauban And Fricourt	25/09/1916	25/09/1916
War Diary	Ville sur Ancre	26/09/1916	27/09/1916
War Diary	St Pierre a Gouy	28/09/1916	28/09/1916
War Diary	Cocquerel	29/09/1916	30/09/1916
War Diary	Ligescourt	30/09/1916	30/09/1916
Heading	War Diary of Headquarters 1st Indian R.H.A. Brigade From 1st October 1916 To 30th October 1916		
War Diary	Ligescourt	02/10/1916	18/10/1916
War Diary	Chateau	19/10/1916	19/10/1916
War Diary	Drucas	19/10/1916	19/10/1916
War Diary	Havernas	20/10/1916	20/10/1916
War Diary	Ligescourt	22/10/1916	02/11/1916
War Diary	St Vallery	04/11/1916	30/11/1916
Heading	War Diary of Headquarters 1st Indian R.H.A. Brigade From 1st December 1916 To 31st December 1916		
Heading	War Diary of Head Quarters. 1st Indian R.H.A. Bde From 1st December 1916 To 31st December 1916 (Volume I		
War Diary	St Valery sur Somme	11/12/1916	31/12/1916

No ap 11/20/11

BEF

1 INDIAN CAV. DIV ~~TROOPS~~

1 ~~INDIAN~~ BDE R.H.A ~~Bde~~

1914 Sept to 1916 Dec

DESIGNATED 16. BDE R.H.F
1916 DEC

TO 4 CAV DIV TROOPS
BOX 1158

WAR DIARY
OF
Head Quarters R.H.A. 1st Indian Cavalry Division.

From 2nd September 1914 to 5th February 1915

includes orders for future operations

HQs RHA 1st Ind Cav Div.

HQs R HA 1st IND. CAV. DIV. I

Army Form O. 2118.

WAR DIARY
or
INTELLIGENCE SUMMARY.
(Erase heading not required.)

Instructions regarding War Diaries and Intelligence Summaries are contained in F. S. Regs., Part II, and the Staff Manual respectively. Title pages will be prepared in manuscript.

Hour, Date, Place.	Summary of Events and Information.	Remarks and references to Appendices.
2nd September 1914	Wire received at Meerut (AG in India 891, 2-9-14 to empower Hd Qrs for Cavalry RHA Cav Div. Personnel taken from 12th Bt RHA Meerut & Horse for D Col Ahmednagar had lastly with Light Horseman Staff Capt St Clair Stranbenzee Orderly Off.	
	Reported Ready	
20th September 1914	Left Meerut encamped Bombay 10th to 8th under Lieut	
9th October 1914	Joined from Ahmednagar	
	Embarked S.S. Ballarat	
13/10/14	Convoy started parted Hd Qrs RHA & U Bty in Ballarat	
16/10/14	A Bty in ITRIR	
	Q " "	
	(from Karachi)	
	B Amta Col	
	C Amta Col	
	E Amta Col	

Army Form O. 2118.

WAR DIARY
or
INTELLIGENCE SUMMARY.

(Erase heading not required.)

Instructions regarding War Diaries and Intelligence Summaries are contained in F. S. Regs., Part II, and the Staff Manual respectively. Title pages will be prepared in manuscript.

Hour, Date, Place.	Summary of Events and Information.	Remarks and references to Appendices.
4th November 1914	Arrived Marseilles. After a good though slow voyage. Hd Qrs CRA Encamped in CHAMPS DE COURSES PARC BURELET. Columns & U Bty encamped LA VALENTINE A & Q Btys in Billets. All units commenced re-equipment, clothing arms &c	
14th November 1914 16 th " "	Left Marseilles by Troop Train Arrived ORLEANS. CRA Hd Qrs in Quartier SONIS 8th Chasseurs Barrack A Bty RHA " Q Btys in Camp at LA SOURCE U " Camp of 40 " - GRUE Columns in Camp of 40 " - GRUE Both Camps very bad, merely a sea of mud Columns (B, C & T) were the first altogether as a Unit. Batteries to finally equipped at ORLEANS. Though MSC Transport was not drawn till arrival in , and being owing to an outbreak of PINKEYE amongst the heavy draught horses from DEPTFORD.	

Army Form C. 2118.

WAR DIARY
or
INTELLIGENCE SUMMARY.

(Erase heading not required.)

Instructions regarding War Diaries and Intelligence Summaries are contained in F. S. Regs., Part II, and the Staff Manual respectively. Title pages will be prepared in manuscript.

Hour, Date, Place.	Summary of Events and Information.	Remarks and references to Appendices.
26th November 1914	Hd Qrs CRA left ORLEANS with Divl HQ in troop train	
28 " "	Arrived at KIMMEL and marched to LOZINGHEM where went into Billets.	
	Batteries Column did not move till todays later owing to the lack of Horse transport due to PINK EYE	
	Batteries now attached to Cav Bdes of RHA Organisation adopted	
	Howrs & Roberts Bdes RHA Hd Qrs remaining attached to Division till further orders	
	Reid Amn Coln at PUCHEL	
	Q Bty at BURBURE	
	A " " ALLOUAGNE	
	U " " LILLIERS	
	Remained in rest area CRA 1st Ind Cav Division appointed OC Divisional Troops	
14th December 1914	Odd Brit troops ordered to be ready to move at an hours notice	
20th " "	Q Bty with C Sec Amn Col ordered forward to BETHUNE and attached to INDIAN ARMY CORPS.	

Army Form C. 2118.

WAR DIARY
or
INTELLIGENCE SUMMARY.

(Erase heading not required.)

IV

Instructions regarding War Diaries and Intelligence Summaries are contained in F. S. Regs., Part II, and the Staff Manual respectively. Title pages will be prepared in manuscript.

Hour, Date, Place.	Summary of Events and Information.	Remarks and references to Appendices.
21st December 1914	SIALKOT CAV BDE also ordered forward, but Q Bty was not taken, only the small arm section of B Section Amn Col.	
22nd " "	One section A Bty in action for short time only June 24 rounds. B.I.C. small arm subsections of columns supplying Bdes etc with S.A.A.	
24 " "	1st Ind Cav Divn is split from INDIAN CAVALRY CORPS (Lt Gen Rimmington) & also moves to new Billeting Area to make room for INDIAN CORPS who are coming back from the trenches. Col LEEKY readbis appointment as CRA 1st Ind Cav Divn & goes to Cav Corps H.Q. as Staff Officer for this. Billeted at BOURECQ with remainder of Divnl H.Q. Divl H.Q. moves to NORRENT FONTES & billets together with Houses BDE. Lt Col ROUSE appointed CRA 1st Ind Cav Divn. A Bty at BEAUMETZ LES AIRES Q Bty at HAUCHIN Q Bty at AUCHY AU BOIS DIV AMN Col at ST HILAIRE & COTTES	

Army Form C. 2118.

WAR DIARY
or
INTELLIGENCE SUMMARY.

(Erase heading not required.)

Instructions regarding War Diaries and Intelligence Summaries are contained in F. S. Regs., Part II, and the Staff Manual respectively. Title pages will be prepared in manuscript.

V

Hour, Date, Place.	Summary of Events and Information.	Remarks and references to Appendices.
25th Dec. 1914	Orders received for Hqrs. 1st I.C.A.C. to move to NORRENT to give more room to the Indian Army Corps. CTA. changed quarters to LA COULEE ½ mile from Divl Hq. in NORRENT	
January 1915	Horses being fit, systematical training carried out. Two divisional exercises being carried out weekly. CTA exercised DIV AMTN COL. 9 DIV AMTN PARK in ammunition supply — and on night of 27th Jan A.Q & O Btys overtook a position by night & entrenched. CTAs staff equipped with a telephone wagon in place of Indian equipment with additional personnel shown in Appendix I.	APPENDIX I Shews alteration in CTAs Staff owing to promotions & new equipment.
31st Jan 1915	During the month A Q & O batteries lost many Officers & NCOs promoted who were mostly sent to join the new Establishment — see the	APPENDIX II Nominal roll of Officers as newly appointed to "A", "Q" & "O" Btys.

Army Form C. 2118.

WAR DIARY
or
INTELLIGENCE SUMMARY.

(Erase heading not required.)

Instructions regarding War Diaries and Intelligence Summaries are contained in F. S. Regs., Part II, and the Staff Manual respectively. Title pages will be prepared in manuscript.

Hour, Date, Place.	Summary of Events and Information.	Remarks and references to Appendices.
January 1915	Batteries were filled with junior ranks & NCOs who had gained experience & obstinaction in the earliest part of the War & promotion amongst the NCOs was rapid. Batteries found they were handicapped being on the Indian Establishment with Indian followers only. being allowed, instead of Batmen. These were represented & being considered by G.H.Q. no extra reserve in DIV. AMTN. COL. owing to their native personnel.	VI
28 Jany 1915	Orders received from 2nd Cav Corps for OCTRHA 30 @ Btys & observing officers (about 15am) to proceed to PRADELLE. 2 Sthlcin officer to get orders as to taking out gun positions from French Batteries which are vacating the trenches. (We being relieved by 5 th Corps (GEN PLUMER)	
29th Jan 15	Orders received at 11.6am for the Division with RHA to be in readiness to move at 2 hrs notice. This cancelled as far as RHA were concerned at 2 P.M. 30th & previous orders to go to PRADELLE held good. OC's arrived by motor at 10 am Btys marching to billets as follows A & C Cavl Amb. 2nd RHA along BOESEGHEM - MORBECQUE road. O Bty

Gulab Singh & Sons, Calcutta.—No. 36 Army C.—29.8.14—1,500 Bks

Serial No. 74.

121/4719

WAR DIARY

OF

R.A. Head Quarters; 1st Indian Cavalry Division.

1st February 1915 – 28th February 1915

From 1st February 1915

WAR DIARY
or
INTELLIGENCE SUMMARY.

(Erase heading not required.)

Army Form C. 2118.

Instructions regarding War Diaries and Intelligence Summaries are contained in F. S. Regs., Part II, and the Staff Manual respectively. Title pages will be prepared in manuscript.

Hour, Date, Place.	Summary of Events and Information.	Remarks and references to Appendices.
	in NOPPENT General GAVE OCTRA 28 Ottoir explained relocation & pointed out probable pos of Btys on Map 20000. BCs reconnoitred the ground with French BCs.	VII
31st Jan 15	GE Q Bty going into old gun pits A&U making fresh pits. BCs back to Btys CO. House in HAZEBROUCK - CRA staff went to Reid Arists Chr.	
	Batteries moved into billets at STRAZEELE. Maj Anto Col BORE Anto Park og PIPPEWE. BCs reconnoitred start observing stns. Orders received for 1 section pair Bty to replace 1 sect French guns in case of "Q" "U" + guns of 13 going up to that new gun position to take place on evening of 1st Feb. Portion of Anti Chr to accompany guns AITN Park moved to join up with 97th Divl Park at move at ST SYLVESTRE. Hqs billeted STRAZEELE. March orders issued for march of RHQ & 28 Btn, Divn Arty to Billets SE of VLAMERTINGHE	
1st Feb 15	Marched at 8am Halting for 10 min of about hours walked all way as transport marched with units.	
12.30p	Arrived in billets where are big farms about 1 mile S of VLAMERTINGHE	

Army Form C. 2118.

WAR DIARY Hqrs. R.A.
or 2nd Cav. Div.
INTELLIGENCE SUMMARY.

(Erase heading not required.)

Hour, Date, Place.	Summary of Events and Information.	Remarks and references to Appendices.
YPRES FEB 6th	Order received to attack. Senior Subaltern of R.H.A. Bty. Lieut Archibald to 28th Divl. Hqrs. Bty - owing to latters inexperience -	Lieut Archibald to 36785 2/Lieut Bates to 6285
FEB 7th	CASUALTY Report 8 am. 2nd Lieut J.H.K. RICHARDSON "Q" Bty. wounded in head. 5 horses Munn. Park ordered to M'BEEK to facilitate ammn. supply.	Lieut Jamieson 6 6985
8th	"U" Battery changed position successfully, but got shelled regularly & had 1 man hit -	
9th	Very still firing - "U" Bty. shelled again. Very quiet. Order received that R.H.A. Btys would be relieved by Belgian Btys - Bs.Cs. accompanying Trek Belgian Majrs to their Hq. found and then Sen.Belgian Majr. to our Govt. Belgian Arty. in charge	
10th	Quiet day. "A" Bty. fires on enemy trenches. Fire reported to be very good Belgian Arty. in charge (latter had very adv. report sent throughly carry out from by 9.20 pm. - Orders to be an AIRE by 13th B. Canal. Belgian Btys. registered & laid wires & telephones to replace our lines - owing to their at BEEBE on night Feb 11 - 12th. - Received	Total Casualties 1 Officer 2 Men } wounded
12th	Btys. and Div. Amn. Clm. marched at 10 am. billeted in town along the STEENVOORDE - L'ABEELE road	2600 horses fed
13th	marched into new billets as follows:-	Stampreye
	Hqrs. R.A., NORRENT FONTES	Stpf Offr R.A.
	"A" Bty. LIERES	(2nd Div)
	"Q" Bty. AUCHY au BOIS	
NORRENT-FONTES	"U" Bty. RELY	
	Amn. Clm. ST HELAIRE	

Army Form C. 2118.

WAR DIARY
or
INTELLIGENCE SUMMARY.
(Erase heading not required.)

Hour, Date, Place.	Summary of Events and Information.	Remarks and references to Appendices.
YPRES. 1st July. 6.10am	Guns moved out of billets & successfully occupied positions BCs taking 1 extra unit wagon — CRA Staff prepared telephone line, & French line which was to be taken over were patrolled — CRA in billets U.9 MERT.N.0.4½ — Wire laid out at 6am from A.B.50 position to the level which CRHA is to take over — 2nd July. French line being used to C & A B.tys telephone line started at Back Yogn. Control brass and the following Daily Reports were made by B.tys reporting lines during the days. 6pm Commander 7pm Remainder of Btys advanced into action & batteries reported successfully — no casualties. CR+A & staff to YPRES, hullaling need Col. BARRIES lieue. Progress reports of Btys shows nothing fired A have an aeroplane action, also C is not in action yet —	CASUALTY REPORT 4.8.M PROGRESS REPORT 5.am 10.P.M 6.P.M
3rd July.	CR+A lost out control of French cares EOA formed not working and one had to be done through BRA station. All men of Staff recognizing one of Btys CRA as many casualties were known to occur. Bty shifting its position by lifting its gun — BU formed account amount of casualties. Lines not working etc. N of YPRES MERT.N 1.0.4.1 Btys fired a round amount of 5 guns were allowed to come into action - Bty fired a round about cycled C.R.H.Bs Staff kit arrived. "A" Bty shelled with Tear Shells jebbing wagon over loaded 9 mile erestractor. "A" Bty shelled with Tear explode.	

Army Form C. 2118.

IX

WAR DIARY
or
INTELLIGENCE SUMMARY.
(Erase heading not required.)

Instructions regarding War Diaries and Intelligence Summaries are contained in F. S. Regs., Part II, and the Staff Manual respectively. Title pages will be prepared in manuscript.

Hour, Date, Place.	Summary of Events and Information.	Remarks and references to Appendices.
YPRES FEB 4th. 31st B.de. 28th Div.	Wires cut to Q & A. Formed either by new infantry cutting brushwood in fences, or spies. O.C. C. reports part of signalling by lamps going on. Intelligence informed. Provost interviewed look out. Col BAPREDO house blown up and left Col KENNY & Rio —*: Given permission to move to another 14yp RFA – A Bty shelled with high explosive. Obtn attack position on a trench in Sq I 34 c took place at night g at 11-30 pm received orders to switch "D" Bty on to a crossroad in I 34 a which was done.	
5th	Report from Infantry that Arty fire has been very effective this was O & Q Btys zone, "17" Bty occupying a new position I 19 g. Q Stn at 4-30pm orders received for Col Towse & Major Eden UP SCAR. These received orders to place 1 gun close up to infantry trench which is to be attacked at 9 pm this evening. Order cancelled at 7-30pm owing to insufficient reconnaissance. Attack took place "D" supported with fire. Results not known*.	

W. W. Smith Capt. Adjt.
[signature] Major Capt.

APPENDIX I

Nominal Roll C.R.A. Staff
1st Ind. Cav. Div.

Officers

Rank	Name	Remarks
Lieut.Col	H Rouse. DSO	C. R. A
Capt.	A.W. VanStraubenzee	Acting Staff Captain

N.C.O's & men

Regt. No.	Rk	Name	Remarks
28256	Sgt	Howell	Appointed from 'U' Bty. R H A. vice Sgt. Campbell
52578	Bdr	Lacy	
35951	"	Morton	} Two R.F.A. men posted as telephonists
735?	"	Thurston	} for telephone cart
53990	Gr	Chappell	C.R.A's Servant
29869	"	Gale	C.R.A's Groom
52068	"	Kent	
62402	"	Roubridge	
13601	"	Roper	
55570	"	Rowe	
22533	Sgt cook	Stone	From Rouse's Bde Staff
51396	ft	Joddering	"
62671	"	Cliff	"
1193	"	Stannard	"
5658?	"	Parker	
43936	"	Samuels	
52798	"	Magee	
96713	"	Goundry	} Joined as R.F.A. telephonists for
96636	"	Penton	} telephone cart
63129	Dr	Fisher	} Drivers of telephone cart joined
72270	"	Cody R A	} from base
16	"	Gammon A S C	G.S. wagon driver

A.W. van Straubenzee
for Staff Capt. R.A.
1st Ind. Cav. Div.

29.1.1915

WAR DIARY   APPENDIX II

Roll of Officers R.H.a 1st Ind Cav Div
                                            1st Feb. 1915.
Brigade Staff

| Lt. Col | H. ROUSE. D.S.O. | |
| Capt | A.W. VAN STRAUBENZEE | |

"M" Battery R.H.a.

Major	R H LASCELLES	
Capt	A.C. ROLLESTON	
Lieut	P.E. INCHBALD D.S.O	
2 "	H.W. HUGGINS	
2 "	A.C. DALE	

"A" Battery R.H.a

Major	A.E. WARDROP	
Capt	H.W. ~~Wynter~~ WYNTER	
Lieut	A.C. BATES	
2 Lieut	R. STAVELEY	
2 Lieut	F. HEATH CALDWELL	

P.T.O.

"Q" Battery R.H.A.

Major	W. R. Eden. D.S.O.
Capt.	H. W. Walker
	J. H. K. Richardson
	G. P. Simpson
	E. S. Howard

Divisional Ammn Col.

Capt.	M. H. McConnel
"	D. C. Wilson
"	J. L. C. White

A96

121/5114

WAR DIARY
OF
With appendices.

Head Quarters R.A. 1st Indian Cavalry Division.
From 1st March 1915 to 31st March 1915.

WAR DIARY Hqrs. R.A. 2nd Ind. Cav. Div.

INTELLIGENCE SUMMARY

Army Form C. 2118.

10

Hour, Date, Place.	Summary of Events and Information.	Remarks and references to Appendices.
NORRENT FONTES 1st March 6.30 p.m.	Order received from G.S. 1st & 2nd Cav. Div. that 3 R.H.A. Btys. and Amm. Colm. (13th Section) were to hold themselves in readiness to move. — Heard unofficially that Lieut. Col. P. Simpson "O" Bty. R.H.A. wounded (now attached to C.R.A. 8th Div.)	
2nd	Instruction received from Cav. Corps that Btys. were to be under C.R.A. VIII Div. and were to march by rug Lt up to their area round LA GORGUE.	
3rd		
4th 8 A.M.	Billeting parties to LA GORGUE and batteries were to march at 2 A.M. Night 4/3-14-14 — Btys. arrived at MERVILLE 6 A.M. went into billets along road running South of the LA BRIANNE — NEUF BERQUIN road — "Q" and "U" Btys. occupied Posns the same evening not close to LA PLINQUE (3/4 mile S. of LAVENTIE) Btys. took awkward posn. in action with them (17.6 yds. in all — Btys. form part of an Horse Arty. Group consisting of A. Q. U. F & T (1st & R.H.A. Bde.) O and Z (5th Bde R.H.A.) all under Col. ROUSE whose Hqrs. were at RUE DE PARADIS.	
LAVANTIE 5th	Q & U Btys. registered on different zone. 2 section D Trenches — "A" Bty. occupied posn. by night S. of RUE BACQUEROT. All Btys. in telephonic cne with Col. ROUSE'S Hqs.	

Army Form C. 2118

WAR DIARY
Hqrs. R.A. 1st Ind. Cav. Div
or INTELLIGENCE SUMMARY.
(Erase heading not required.)

Instructions regarding War Diaries and Intelligence Summaries are contained in F. S. Regs., Part II, and the Staff Manual respectively. Title pages will be prepared in manuscript.

Hour, Date, Place.	Summary of Events and Information.	Remarks and references to Appendices.
6th March 1915 LAVANTIE - RUE DE PARADIS.	A.Q. 20' registered - A" being fired at at once stopped as they are 1200 yds. from German lines and dug a new position in the evening - Conference of Col.s at 9." Div. Hqrs. R.A.	
7th March	A" & D" again registered on a zone further E. and fresh ground unaltered E. of NEUVE CHAPELLE - Catered situation unchanged -	
8th March	Div. Arty. Cav. moved back to E. in HAVERSKERQUE - Except 17. 4th Div. and is now so further N. than our Corps. General situation unchanged. Orders for attack on NEUVE CHAPELLE by 8th Dn. and a further advance on to AUBERS - LA CLIQUETERIE issued - See appendix III	× APPENDIX II
9th March		APPENDIX 3
13th March 7.40 am	1st Phase of Artillery fire commenced - See appendix III no movement of enemy reported. A heavy morning -	
8.10 am	2nd Phase of Arty. fire commenced see appendix III	
8.45 am	3rd Phase of Arty. fire commences.	
	Rele. of fire & advance of section fire 5 min. for H.Q.V.	
9.30 - 10.30 am	No Reps recd from friend observing Officer that trouble in NEUVE CHAPELLE has been taken them from line being shown by VERY'S lights - Amn. wagons come up into a position N. of RUE de BOIS - Div. Amn. Col.	
12 noon	18 Amn. wagons 1 from Div. Amn. Column respectively Main body 17 In Div. went into fresh billets at In BRIONNE	

Army Form C. 2118

WAR DIARY
H.Q. S.R.A. of 1ST IND. CAV. DIV.
INTELLIGENCE SUMMARY.
(Erase heading not required.)

Instructions regarding War Diaries and Intelligence Summaries are contained in F. S. Regs., Part II, and the Staff Manual respectively. Title pages will be prepared in manuscript.

Hour, Date, Place.	Summary of Events and Information.	Remarks and references to Appendices.
LAVENTIE RUE DE PARADIS 10th March 3.30 pm	8th Div. Inf. attack apparently successful. 7th Div. attack commenced. Supplied Vry. our fire for this A.G.V. C.R.A. 8th Div.	not appendix no 3. 2 Lieutenant J.G. BROWN attached to 9 Rly acc'dntly injured reported as a casualty. Btys fired S.A. 696 6"H. 696 10"H. 557? Appendix 4 A Tug RP fires for 10th 11th
11th March 6 pm	Rlys. ordered to start firing. 8th Div. attack proposed to 9th div @ 1st T.2.E. by 6.30pm.	
4 am	Orders received for attack bombardment and attack at 7am by 9th Div. Appendix IV B	Ammon expended 11th A - 599 Q - 459 U - 472
6.45 am	Bombardment commenced	
7 am	attack - misty morning - but much mudd. Lines shifted very little all day un evening infantry here at advanced. 21st BE reported missing Intno. definite information	X R.S. PATKERSON of 62nd Bty. R.F.A attached Q Rty RHA - 429 A " - 589 " - 369
5 pm	Night lines issued for H.A. groups. Appendix V	Appendix 5 A A - 369 Q - 443 U - 254
11.45 pm	Orders issued for attack tomorrow. Appendix VI	
12th (88)	Misty. Att. Bombardment postponed to 9.50 am Btys fired on communication trenches all day after Sun late (1 fire - infantry decupied by 7 pm. (150) (101)	
13th	Btys on night lines.	
(88) (83)	Orders for attack postponed. attacked	
	During morning F.O.O's. A and Q observed fire for 6" & 4.5" Howitzers bombardment reported Successful. V. Bty. 2 casualties.	
14th 12. 3.0 am 7 am 7 pm	After fee enid (Appendix VII). Instructions not to engage enemy guns for a quiet day. Btys chiefly engaged enemy batteries (Appendix VII) Night lines as for last ing lt	A - 176 Q - 198 U - 1118

Army Form C. 2118

13

WAR DIARY
1st IND. CAV. DIV.
INTELLIGENCE SUMMARY.
(Erase heading not required.)

Instructions regarding War Diaries and Intelligence Summaries are contained in F. S. Regs., Part II, and the Staff Manual respectively. Title pages will be prepared in manuscript.

Hour, Date, Place.	Summary of Events and Information.	Remarks and references to Appendices.
MARCH 15th RUE DE PARADIS - LAVENTIE 6 AM	Batteries on lines as viewed by Appendix VIII - Moving forward	Appendix VI
7. P.M.	Night lines as for 15th - Headquarters Park, Rieulle	A = 5, 6 Q = 3, 4 J = 3 & 9 Moved first
16th 9 A.M.	Day lines as for 15th	A = 2, 6 Q = 5 J = 2, 9
3.30.	Lines extended [Front line park] 106 to 133. One wire from "A" Bty to Coy. HQ. Royal Welsh Fusiliers and another from 111th R.G.A. with Queens Reg't. and another from 111th R.G.A. built with R.G.A. (F.D.F.) and 14th Brigade	
17th 12.30 P.M.	Group reorganised - consists of Adorn. - 14th Brigade	Supplement Div. Arty. Orders
23rd	"A" Battery Registered 9 fresh points. 20th Inf. Bde. Relief of 23 and Inf. Bde. occupied their old lines.	Heavies have a G.L. Wagon [?] of Ranville to replace [?] [?] now in position.
24th	"U" Battery Registered 4 fresh points.	The 13th Inf. Bde. has [?] in [?] in
29th	"A" Bty. Change of position to ÉPINETTE on former position and to accurately marked unchanged as before.	[?] of the 7th Div. Lists have gone through [?] of the battery will [?] with R.S.F.E. on R.H.A. on Rotts with 1 PM & Co. Bty.
30th	"A" Bty registered from new position. General distribution unchanged - very little firing owing to enemy's [?] of ammunition [?] on arrival [?] in R.G.A. R.H.A. [?] on a mobile Routine and Hqrs. Reg. unchanged. Com... up to this date with M.G.D.	A.W.[?] [?] to [?] [?]

APPENDIX II

(1) Copy No. 16

INSTRUCTIONS FOR ACTION
8th Division and attached Artillery.

Reference Maps - Belgium and France Sheet 36 S.W. $\frac{1}{20,000}$
and NEUVE CHAPELLE $\frac{1}{5,000}$

9-3-15.

1. The 4th and Indian Corps are to carry out a vigorous attack on the enemy ~~on a date and at an hour to be notified later.~~ tomorrow at 8-5 am.
The first objective is the capture of NEUVE CHAPELLE, after which a further advance will be made to gain the line AUBERS - LE PLOUICH - LA CLIQUETERIE FERME - LIGNY LE GRAND.

2. The attack on the village of NEUVE CHAPELLE will be carried out in two stages by the 8th Division.

   First Objective - The enemy's front and support trenches opposite "B" lines.

   Second Objective - Eastern edge of NEUVE CHAPELLE village on the right to ORCHARD No.6, and the MOATED GRANGE on the left.
   The point of junction with the Indian Corps will be at the S.E. corner of the Village Point No.80

   The INDIAN CORPS will make a simultaneous attack on NEUVE CHAPELLE from the SOUTH.

3. For the attack on NEUVE CHAPELLE village, the Artillery of the 7th and 8th Divisions, less the 4.7" Heavy Batteries, will be grouped under the orders of the G.O.C. 8th Division; the 4.7" batteries of the 7th and 8th Divisions together with certain heavy batteries will form a group under the orders of 1st Army.

4. The 23rd and 25th Infantry Brigades will carry out the attack of the 8th Division until the capture of the village is completed.
The 25th Infantry brigade will be on the RIGHT and the 23rd Infantry Brigade on the LEFT.
The dividing line between the brigades will be the road (14) (17) (18) (19) (31) for which the left brigade will be responsible.

5. The action of the 8th Division and attached artillery to support this attack will be as laid down in table of tasks already issued to all concerned.

No.5 MOUNTAIN BATTERY.

No 5 MOUNTAIN BATTERY (less 1 section) will accompany the Right attack and act under the orders of the G.O.C. 35th Infantry Brigade.

1 Section No.5 MOUNTAIN BATTERY will accompany the left attack and act under the orders of the G.O.C. 23rd Infantry Brigade.

6. POSITION OF WAGON LINES.

During the attack on NEUVE CHAPELLE the position of the Gun and Wagon teams will be as follows:-

1st Indian Cavalry Division Artillery) 5th Brigade, R.H.A.)	M 3 b
2nd Indian Cavalry Division Artillery)	R 6 d
22nd Brigade, R.F.A.	R 6 c
35th Brigade, R.F.A.	R 5 d
33rd Brigade, R.F.A.	M 1 d and M 2 a
45th Brigade, R.F.A.	M 2 a, M 2 b, M 2 c
57th Field Howitzer Brigade, R.F.A.	L 34 d and G 32 b (31st Battery).

All other teams of the remainder of the Artillery units will remain with their respective wagon lines.

(3)

7. Bombing Parties will mark their position in captured trenches by blue signalling flags.

The Grenadiers of the INDIAN CORPS are using Pink flags for the same purpose.

During their advance the Infantry will indicate their position as they get forward by the use of VEREYS lights.

8. Regimental Aid Posts will be established at following places.

(a) Four hundred yards SOUTH of ROUGE CROIX (M 27 b) on LA BASSEE Road.

(b) "C" lines Headquarters M 22 central

(c) "D" lines Headquarters M 23 a.

Advanced dressing stations on LA BASSEE road one mile SOUTH of railway crossing M 8 b.
This will also be used as a Divisional Collecting Station to which wounded men, able to walk should be directed.

9. Headquarters R.A. 8th Division will remain in its present position.

R H Johnson Major. R.A.
Brigade Major 8th Division Artillery.

Issued at 4.45 pm

APPENDIX III

The accompanying tasks for the attack on NEUVE CHAPELLE are forwarded.

All previous instructions on this subject are to be destroyed.

These instructions and tasks are to be treated as SECRET and be carefully safeguarded.

The Bombardment for the 1st Phase lasts 30 minutes in the case of the Siege batteries, with the exception of 5th Siege which fires for 35 minutes, and for 25 minutes in the case of Horse and Field Guns and Howitzers, when the first lift takes place.

The Bombardment for the 2nd Phase similarly lasts for 30 minutes where the second lift takes place and the 3rd Phase commences.

The 3rd Phase continues until we have consolidated ourselves in the enemy's position.

Tasks for covering any subsequent advance will be allotted later.

Although tasks and times are allotted and these (especially the times) are to be rigidly adhered to, until orders for a change are issued; it is always the unexpected which happens in War and Battery Commanders must be prepared for both change of tasks and for being kept longer on certain zones or brought back to zones which they have quitted.

These changes depend on the information received during the action, and all ranks must be prepared for these changes

RHJohnson

Major. R.A.

Brigade Major 8th Divisional Artillery.

1st PHASE

		The Bombardment	30 Minutes	Ammunition deemed sufficient.
5 Siege Battery	A M A M 8.0 to 8.20 8.21 to 8.35	Post (27) Trench (33) to (34)		30 rounds per gun
6 Siege Battery	8.5 to 8.20 8.21 to 8.35	Trench (27) to (37) Trench (34) to (72)		do.
Siege Battery M 15 c	8.5 to 8.20 8.21 to 8.35	Trench (72) to (74) Trench (38) to (82)	(1 Section on (17) from 8.21 – 8.35)	do.
4 Siege Battery	8.5 to 8.20 8.21 to 8.35	Trench (74) to (76) Trench (82) to (75)	Front trench Rear trench	do.
Siege Battery M 10 a	8.5 to 8.20 8.21 to 8.35	Trench (76) to (20) Trench (75) to (77)		do.

4.5" Howitzers

35 Battery R.F.A.	A M A M 8.10 to 8.35	(58) to (40)	1 section on (27)	40 rounds per gun
55 do.	8.10 to 8.35	(40) to (41)		do.
31 do.	8.10 to 8.35	(75) to (77)		do.

1st Phase (Continued)

13 and 18 Pounders.

	A.M.	A.M.		Ammunition deemed sufficient
"A" Group				
3rd and 45th Brigades.	8.0 to 8.15		Wirecutting 200ˣ at (15) and 75ˣ SOUTH + 150ˣ NORTH of road (34)	40 rounds per gun
3rd Brigade (14 Guns)	8.16 to 8.35		(27) to (17) and search back 400ˣ	
45th Brigade (22 guns)	8.16 to 8.35		(17) to (20) and search back 400ˣ	20 rounds per gun
"B" Group				
2 Batteries 22nd Brigade	8.5/ to 8.35		Trench (33) to (44) and trenches (58) to (70) and (69) to (71)	20 rounds per gun H.E.
1 Battery 22nd Brigade	8.5/ to 8.35		(27) and search back 300ˣ	20 rounds per gun Shrapnel to search
35th Brigade	8.5/ to 8.35		(33) to (17) and search back 400ˣ	10 rounds per gun H.E.
				20 rounds per gun Shrapnel to search.
"X" and "Y" Batteries	8.5/ to 8.35		Search roads running into BOIS DU BIEZ at (36) (97) and (98)	30 rounds per gun
"N" Battery		8.5/ to 8.35	area (7) (3) (4)	do.
118th Heavy Battery	8.25 to 8.35		Post (27)	10 rounds per gun
"Z" and "O" Batteries	7.45 8.5/to 8.35		Area (7) (3) (4)	30 rounds per gun
"A" "Q" "U" Batteries	8.5/to 8.35		Bursts of fire on "A", (86), (94), (98), search and sweep	30 rounds per gun
"F" and "T" Batteries	8.5/to 8.35		Trench (3) to (4)	20 rounds per gun
				20 rd do.

NOTE. On all occasions when shelling troops under cover, one section should fire High Explosive if such ammunition is available.

2nd PHASE.   30 Minutes Bombardment.

6" Howitzers

	A.M. to A.M.		Ammunition deemed sufficient
5th Siege Battery	8.35 to 9.5	NEUVE CHAPELLE area (62) (32)	30 rounds per gun
6th Siege Battery	8.35 to 9.5	do do	do.
4th Siege Battery	8.35 to 9.5	(19) and trenches 150X to NORTH of it	do.
Siege Battery M 15 c	8.35 to 9.5	(5) and trench 75X on either side of it	do.
Siege Battery M 10 a	8.35 to 9.5	(4) and 150X of trench to SOUTH of it	do.

4.5" Howitzers

35th Battery	8.35 to 9.5	Trench (47), 6 (22) and Cross roads (18)	30 rounds per gun
51st Battery	8.35 to 9.5	Post (6) and trenches (4) to (3)	20 do.
55th Battery	8.35 to 9.5	Trenches EAST of road (18) to (66)	30 do.

13 and 18 Pounders

Wirecutting Group	A.M. to A.M.		
32nd and 33rd Batteries	8.35 to 9.5	(62) to (25) and search back 300X	30 rounds per gun
36th Battery R.F.A.	8.35 to 9.5	Trench (2) to (3) and search back 400X	do.
45th Brigade R.F.A.	8.35 to 9.5	From (19) to 400X SOUTH and search back 400X	do.

"B" Group

22nd Brigade, R.F.A.	8.35 to 9.5	(57) to (65) and search back 400X	40 rounds per gun
35th Brigade, R.F.A.	8.35 to 9.5	(18) to (67) and search back 400X	do.
"N", "K" and "W"	8.35 to 9.5	(6) to (9) and search back 400X	do.

Horse Artillery Group.

| "O" and "Z" batteries | 8-5 8-35 8.35 to 9.5 | (79) to (4) and search back 300X | |
| "A" "Q" "U" "P" and "T" | 8.35 to 9.5 | Bursts of fire on "A", (85), (94) (98) search and sweep | 20 rounds a gun |

NOTE.   On all occasions when shelling troops under cover one section should fire High Explosive if such ammunition is available.

3rd PHASE after trench is taken.

6" Howitzers.

			Ammunition deemed sufficient.
5th Siege Battery	(97)	)	
6th Siege Battery	(98)	)	These points to be
4th Siege Battery N 15 c.	)	) on trenches (2) to MOULIN de PIETRE road	shelled periodically and watched.
Siege Battery N 10 a.	)	)	

4.5" Howitzers.

35th Battery	(94)	30 rounds per gun
55th Battery	(86)	do.
53rd Battery	Point "A"	do.

13 and 18 Pounders.

"A" Group.

32nd)		
33rd) Batteries	Watch front (30) to (31) and search back 400ˣ	40 rounds per gun
1st)		

3rd)		
5th) Batteries	Watch front (5) to (3) and search back 400ˣ	40 rounds per gun
36th)		

"B" Group.

"F", "Y", "A"	Watch front (31) to (5) and search back 400ˣ	40 rounds per gun
22nd Brigade R.F.A.	Watch front (30) to (31) and search back 400ˣ	do.
55th Brigade R.F.A.	Watch front (5) to (3) and search back 400ˣ	do.

H.A. Group.   H.A. batteries will continue on zone "A", (86), (98), (96), and (94) — 40 rounds per gun.

NOTE.   On all occasions when shelling troops under cover one section should fire High Explosive if such ammunition is available.

Appendix III

1st Phase. The Bombardment 30 mins. Ammn. deemed Sufficient

'Z' & 'O' Btys	7.40 am. to 8.5 am.	Area (7) (3) (4)	30 Rds. per gun.
'A' Q & 'U' Btys	" " " "	{ Bursts of fire on "A", (86), (94) } (98) search & sweep	20 Rds. per gun
F & T Btys	" " " "	Trench (3) to (4)	20 Rds. per gun.

2nd Phase. 30 mins bombardment.

Horse Artillery Group

O & Z Btys.	8.5 am. to 8.35 am.	(79) to (4) & search back 300ˣ	20 Rds. per Gun
'A' 'Q' & 'U' F & T Btys	" " " "	Bursts of fire on 'A', (86), (94) (98) search & Sweep	20 Rds. per Gun

3rd Phase. After Trench is taken.

H.A. Group.   H.A. Btys. will continue on Zone 'A', (86), (98), (96) & (94)   40 Rds. per gun.

App. 4A

Prefix	Code	m.	Words	Charge	(X) For Stamps	Rec'd. at ___ 19
Office of Origin and Service Instructions. APPENDIX 4A			Sent. At ___ m. To ___ By ___		IV H	Date ___ From ___ By ___

NOTHING TO BE WRITTEN BY THE ADDRESSOR ABOVE THIS LINE.

TO (See instructions on back.)	O	A	C Q	U	
* Sender's Number.	Day of Month. 18		In reply to number.		AAA

21st Infantry Bde. now holds position left resting on GERMAN trench M29B central thence to road ough M30C thence South to border to (M36 A central) AAA Three trains arrived at WAVRIN AAA Night attack most probable AAA attack from PIETRE may develop during night AAA Night lines will be laid as follows:
A BTY on 144 (M36 B 8 4)
U BTY on 143 (N 25 C 4 2)
O BTY on 113
Z BTY on track running N.W from N.E. exit from AUBERS

FROM Place ___ Time ___

(Y) The above may be forwarded as now corrected. (Z) 57   Class of Message.

Countersignature of Censor or Authorising Officer.   Signature of addressor and his instructions, vide reverse.

* This line should be erased if not required.

Army Form C. 2121.

Q Bty on RUE DELAVAL
14th Bde. RHA one bty. on
track running S.E from Farm
DELEVAL and one bty. on
track running S.E from
ROUGE BANCS. AAA

A. U and D Btys. to be prepared
to concentrate on 144 AAA
receipt of

A. Bty. will fire four times before
4 AM on 144 AAA using
15 rounds per bty. on each
occasion

Please acknowledge

FROM: HF GROUP

Appendix IV A.

To   'A' 'Q' & 'U' Btys.

10.3.15.

21st Infantry Bde. now holds position left resting on GERMAN trench M 29 B Centre, thence to road angle M 30 C, thence South to (M 36 A Centre) AAA. Three trains arrived at WAVRIN AAA. Night attack most probable AAA.

Attack from PIETRE may develop during night AAA. Night lines will be laid as follows:-

'A' Bty on 144 (M 36 B 8 4)
'U' Bty on 143 (N 25 C 4 2)
'O' Bty on 113
'Z' Bty on track running N.W. from N.E. exit from AUBERS.

'Q' Bty. on RUE DELAVAL

14th. Bde. R.H.A. One Bty. on track running S.E. from Farm DELAVAL and one Bty. on track running S.E. from ROUGE BANCS AAA.

'A' 'U' & 'O' Btys to be prepared to concentrate on 144 AAA.

'A' Bty. will fire four times before 4 a.m. on 144. AAA. Using 15 Rounds per battery on each occasion.

Please acknowledge.

from   H.A. Group.

App 4B

"A" Form.   Army Form C. 2121.
MESSAGES AND SIGNALS.   No. of Message

TO: APPENDIX IV B

Day of Month: 11/3/15   AAA

INSTRUCTIONS for VII DIVISIONAL and attached Arty.

Ref. 1/8000 and Numbered Trench Map and
1/20,000 Sheet 36 S.W. FRANCE.

① The 7th Divn. is to continue the attack of AUBERS today.

② The first Objective of 21st Inf. Bde. will be PIETRE – MOR DU PIETRE road, against which it will advance at 7 am.

③ At 6.45 am the artillery will bombard its first Objective.

Ⓒ RFA group 105 to 119 searching back to RIVIERE DES LAYES.

④ Fire on first objectives will cease at 7 am unless otherwise ordered.

"A" Form.
MESSAGES AND SIGNALS.

(5) Orders will then be issued from this office as to time of opening fire on SECOND OBJECTIVE which will be as follows:-

(c) R.H.A Group as for first objectives, para (c)③ but guns therein detailed to fire on ⑤ ⑥ will now search ⑫ to ⑭. and no fire will be applied W. of ⑥.

(6) During this phase the right batteries of the R.H.A. group must carefully watch the progress of the left of the 21st Inf. Bde. as it advances on LES MOTTES.

(7) THIRD OBJECTIVES will be engaged as when ordered as under:-

"A" Form.
MESSAGES AND SIGNALS.
Army Form C. 2121.

(7) (C) R.H.A. Group 1 Brigade ROE DELEVAL. Remainder search area between N & S. Hads of AUBERS.

(9) Rate of fire for first Objective (15 min bombardment) ammunition is allowed as follows:—
13 prs. 15 rds. per gun.

(10) Hqs. 7 D.A. remain as at present.

(11) All telephone lines must be constantly patrolled and immediately repaired when necessary.

All Brigades and Groups will call up HQ. at least once every hour.

sd S.W. Rawlins Maj RA
B de Major 7th D.A.

APPENDIX IV B   B.M. 22.
                 11/3/15

Instructions for VIIth Divisional and Attached Artillery

Ref 1/19000 numbered French map.

1. The VII Division is to continue the attack of AUBERS today.

2. The first objective of XXI Inf Bde will be the PIETRE – MIN DE PIETRE road, against which it will advance at 7. am.

3. At 6.45 am the artillery will bombard its

FIRST OBJECTIVE

(a) 7th Siege Group

   1 Siege Bty – road 102 – 103.
   1 Siege Bty }
   31st How Bty } 86
   1 Siege Bty   104 + along communication trenches up to RIVIERE DES LAYES.

   NOTE. The Siege battery detailed to fire on 86 will register that point, if possible, between 6. am and 6.45 am.

(b) 35th F.A. Bde
                 146 – to 105

(c) R.H.A. group.
                 105 to 119, searching back to RIVIERE DES LAYES

(d) 22 F.A. Bde
                 TRIVELET to 125, inclusive, and searching back to RIVIERE DES LAYES.

4. Fire on First Objectives will cease at 7 am. unless otherwise ordered.

5. Orders will then be issued from this office as to time of opening fire on
SECOND OBJECTIVES

2.

5. Continued.
SECOND OBJECTIVES,
which will be as follows:-

(a) 7th Siege Group
    1 Siege Bty on LES MOTTES Farm.
    2 Siege Batteries - on 113 + houses S.E. of it.
    31st How Bty - area 118, 119, 120, 121.

(b) 35 Bde RFA
    143 to 112.

(c) R.H.A. group
    as for first objectives, para 3c, but guns therein detailed to fire 105-106 will now search 112 to 114. and no fire will be applied west of 106.

(d) 22 Brigade RFA
    as for first objectives para 3.d.

(6) During this phase the right batteries of the R.H.A. group must carefully watch the progress of the left of XXI Inf Bde as it advances on LES MOTTES Farm.

(7) THIRD OBJECTIVES will be engaged when ordered as under :-

(a) 7th Siege Group.
    1 Siege Bty. - 200
    1 Siege Bty - 115 + 116.
    1 Siege Bty - NORTH road of AUBERS
    31 How Bty - SOUTH road of AUBERS

(b) 35 Bde RFA
    200 to 115.

(c) R.H.A. group.
    1 Bde   RUE DELAVAL
    Remainder search area between N + S roads of AUBERS.

(d) 22 Bde. RFA   Area 127, 129, 130, 133.

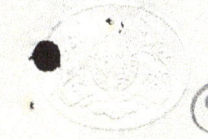

(8) Ammunition.

The Siege Batteries will employ heavy Lyddite as long as ranges admit

(9) Rate of Fire

For 1st Objectives (15 mins bombardment) ammunition is allowed as follows

13 + 18 Pdr Batteries   15 rounds per gun.
Siege Batteries   5   "   "   "
31st How Bty   7   "   "   "

(10) HQS. 7. D.A. remain as at present.

(11) All telephone lines must be constantly patrolled and immediately repaired when necessary. All Brigades and Groups will call up Head Quarters at least once every hour.

SW Marshis
Maj. R.A.
Brigade Maj. 7. D.A.

Issued at 12.45 am to

1 R.H.A. group.
3 Siege group.
5 35th F.A. Bde.
4 22nd F.A. Bde.

Copies to 7 Div. + 8th Div Arty
         2   9

6.7.8 retained

Appendix IV B.

11.3.15

Instructions for R.H.A. Group in compliance with
7th D A Instructions.

FIRST OBJECTIVE ③Ⓒ

H.A. Group will fire on the zone TRIVELET — Road elbow N19C 32 — MOULIN DE PIETRE.
Batteries will divide this zone in the following order:—
'A', 'U', 'O', 'Z', 'Q', 14th Bde. R.H.A.. 'A' Bty. will direct its fire on MOULIN DE PIETRE, 'Q' Bty. on road elbow N19C32, left battery 14th Bde. on TRIVELET. Remaining Btys. dividing the front. All btys. will search from RIVIERE DES LAYES back to within safe distance of our trenches. Rate of fire Section fire 30 seconds.

Second Objective.

'A' & 'U' Btys search RUE D'ENFER from LES MOTTES FARM to 200 yards S.E. of the cross roads S.E. of LES MOTTES FARM. Remaining batteries as for first objective, 'O' Bty. being careful not to fire W. of ⑩⑥ vide §5Ⓒ 7th Divn Instructions Attention of all is drawn to §6 of those instructions Rate of fire Section Fire 2 minutes.

Third Objective 14th Bde. R.H.A. RUE DE LAVAL

Remaining batteries await orders.
Watches will be synchronized with H.A. Group at 6 am. Sd. A Main Capt RHA
H.A. Group.

App V.

"A" Form.   Army Form C. 2121.
MESSAGES AND SIGNALS.   No. of Message 111

TO: OC's Batteries

Day of Month: Eleventh

Night lines will be laid out as follows AAA 'A' Battery on PIETRE cross-roads M36b AAA 'V' road junction N25C 53 AAA 'Q' cross-roads N25 b 25 AAA 14th Brigade track running N.N. from N.E. corner of AUBERS one battery and TRIVELET one battery AAA. O & Z Batteries may move during the night but pending move will be laid with centre lines on PIETRE Please acknowledge.

A. Mann

From: H.A. Group
Place: 6.50 p.m.

Appendix V

To   OC's Batteries.
              Eleventh/3/15.
Night lines will be laid out as follows AAA.
'A' Bty on PIETRE Cross Roads M 366 AAA
'O' Bty Road junction N25 C 53 AAA.
Q Bty Cross Roads N25 B 25 AAA
14th Bde RAA back running N.W. from Corner
of AUBERS one Battery & TRIVELET one
battery AAA. 'O' & 'Z' Btys. may move during
the night but pending move will be laid
with centre lines on PIETRE.
                    Please acknowledge.
              Signed A. Hain Capt RAA
                HA. Group.   6.50 pm.

MESSAGES AND SIGNALS.

Army Form C. 2121.

APPENDIX 5A

Day of Month: 13

AAA

Instructions in compliance with
Div. Arty. 8th Div. Instns.
(i). With reference to (5 d)
A' Bty will fire on front line trenches
running NW and parallel to 105 (104)
up to road.
(ii) The cmn: trenches running to 104 & 105
and bag house.
14th Bde cmn. trenches up to 141
Rate of fire Section fire 1/min.
(8 d)   A & U   106, 107, 108
          Q   110, 111, 112
          14th Bde. 108, 109, 111, 112
Rate of fire Section fire 5 min.
10. OC 14th Bde to detach an
Offr as FOO to —
Watches synchronised at 7 AM with
HA Comp.

From: HA Comp.
Time: 4.45 AM

Appendix VA

Instructions for VII Divisional and attached artillery
for 13th March 1915.

Maps.
Ref. 1/40,000
& Numbered
Trench map
1/10,000

(1) Our infantry are approximately on the line (100) to 101 to road elbow near 88 — (85)

(2) The 8th. Div. is to capture the houses about 88 – 86 during the night 12/13th

(3) The 7th. Division will continue its advance on the objectives already allotted.

(4) The artillery will prepare the advance, opening fire at 9.0 am. and continuing bombardment till 9.40 a.m., when bombardment will stop. The infantry will begin to advance at 9.30 am. but will wait if, as they approach their objectives, the artillery has not yet ceased firing.

(5) Tasks are allotted to artillery as follows:—

(d) R.H.A. Group.
The front line and communication trenches leading to Big House – 104 105 141.

(8) At 9.40 am., immediately after the bombardment, artillery will begin a slow rate of fire on objectives as under.

(d) R.H.A Group.
106 – 107 – 110 – 112 & 108 – 109.
A&U   A&U   Q   A&U
111 – 112

Fire on these ~~trenches~~ objectives will be continued till further orders, while the infantry consolidate their position.

Appendix V A.

13.3.15

Instructions in Compliance with Divl: Arty. 8th Div. Insns.

(1) With reference to (5d)
'A' Bty. will fire on front line trenches running N.W. and parallel to (105)(104) up to road
'Q' & 'U' The cme. trenches running [struck] to 104 & 105 and big house.
14th Bde Cme: trenches up to 141.
Rate of fire Section fire / minute.

(8d) 'A' & 'U' 106, 107, 108.
      'Q'   110, 111, 112.
      14th Bde 108, 109, 111, 112
Rate of fire Section fire 5 minutes.

(10) O.C. 14th Bde. to detail the Officer referred to.
Watches synchronised at 7 a.m. with H.A. Group.

H.A. Group.   4.45 A.m.

APPENDIX VA

BM. 42

Instructions for VII Divisional & attached artillery for 13th March 1915.

Maps
Ref 1/40,000.
+ Numbered Trench
Map 1/10,000

(1) Our infantry are approximately on the line (100) – 101 – road Elbow near 88 – (85)

(2) The 8th Div is to capture the houses about 88 – 86 during the night 12/13th.

(3) The 7th Division will continue its advance on its objectives already allotted.

20 Inf Bde. is to capture the houses near M^m Mir du PIETRE, and also those about 88; if the latter are not captured by 8th Div

21st Inf Bde. is to capture the houses and road — Big House near 102 – 102 – 103 – – road Elbow. Moulin du PIETRE, and the trenches beyond, Nos. 104 + 105.

(4) The artillery will prepare the advance, opening fire at 9.0 am. and continuing bombardment till 9.40 am (when firing bombardment will stop). The infantry will begin to advance at 9.30 am, but will wait if, as they approach their objectives, the artillery has not yet ceased firing.

(5) Tasks are allotted to artillery as follows

(a) 7th Siege Group

Big house – 102 – 103 and road Elbow – houses near M^m MOULIN DU PIETRE

O.C. 7th Siege Group will distribute the fire of his four batteries as he thinks best paying special attention to the BIG HOUSE. At 9.30 am he will direct the fire of 4 guns on to the trench 103 – 104. and the fire of 4 more guns on the trench 105 – 104.

5 cont.

    b. 35 F.A. Bde.

        26 Bty — Big House

        12 } Btys — houses near M in MOULIN
        58 }   DU PIETRE.

    c. 22 F.A. Bde

        104 Bty — houses near M in
                        MOULIN DU PIETRE

    d. R.H.A. Group

        The front line and communication trenches leading to Big House – 104 105 141.

6. The remainder of the 22 F.A. Bde will be ready to engage any targets presented by the bombardment or in front of E & F trenches.

7. Early today and previous to the bombardment O.C. 35 F.A. Bde will arrange to blow a large gap in the enemy's front parapet at 106.
The object of this is that the 22 Inf. Bde shall place a machine gun covering this gap so as to fire on any enemy infantry moving along trench towards 105.

8. At 9.40 am, immediately after the bombardment, artillery will begin a slow rate of fire on objectives as under

    (a) 7th Siege Group
        1 battery on 143.
        1 battery on 115
        1 battery on 113
        1 battery on LES MOTTES FARM.

b 35 F.A. Bde   141 - 143

c 22 FA Bde   TRIVELET

d R.H.A Group.
106-107 - 110 - 112 + 108-109.
111 - 112.

Fire on these objectives will be continued till further orders, while the infantry consolidate their positions

9. Notwithstanding the foregoing instructions the whole of the artillery will be prepared to turn fire at any moment during the day onto any hostile counter attack that may develop.

10. OC. RHA group will detail an officer to be with HQs XX Inf Bde during the day; OC. 35 F.A. Bde an officer to be with HQs. XXI Inf Bde.
These officers to be in telephonic communication with their artillery brigades.

11. Ammunition deemed sufficient for the bombardment.
Howitzer Batteries 20 rounds per gun.
18 Pdr Batteries 60 rounds .. ..
13 Pdr .. 60 .. .. ..

Issued at 2.am. 13/3/15
Copies to 7th Div
20th Inf. Bde
21st Inf Bde
RHA Group
22. FA Bde
35 F.A. Bde
Siege group.

SWH Lawkins
Maj. RA.
Brigade Major
7th DA

SECRET   VI   B.M. 30

Instructions for VII Divisional and attached Artillery
for 12th March 1915

Ref. Maps
1/40,000
1/10,000
(numbered
Trench)

1. Our Infantry hold the line 1-2-90-89 up towards 86, approximately
2. Two Bat^{ns} ~~XX~~ 4th Infy B^{de} are to attack the area - road elbow by MOULIN DE PIETRE - 103 - 102 - 101 - 100 - 99 - big house north west of 102 - 105 - 104.
3. The attack will be preceded by 40 minutes bombardment which will begin at 9.50 am.
4. The 35th F.A. B^{de} (2 Batteries in RUE du BACQUEROT and one battery in M.20.D) will bombard the area of attack with Shrapnel & H.E. The fire of this Brigade will include the Quadrilateral between our original trenches and the line 99-100. That is to say the front ~~of area~~ to be bombarded now extends from 99 to 105. Ammunition considered sufficient 80 rounds per gun.
5. 7th Siege Group will bombard the area of attack as follows
    1 Battery on Quadrilateral between our original trenches and 99-100
    1 Battery on big house and search back to road elbow
    1 Battery on big house
    31st How^r Battery, 1 section on communication trench 99, 1 on 100-101, one on big house - 103. Ammunition considered sufficient 30 rounds per gun.
5.a. At 10.30 am the infantry will assault
At this hour all bombarding guns will concentrate on the area 100-101-103-104-105-Big house ~~front 103-105~~, and will not fire north west of 100-101
At 10.40 am bombardment ceases, except that the battery 35th F.A. B^{de} in M.20.D. will search up to 141 for another 10 minutes

APPENDIX VI

→

2.

(6) In addition to those batteries actually bombarding the area of attack, the remaining artillery will assist the attack by their fire as follows:—

(a) ~~7th Siege Group~~
  ~~[struck out]~~

(b) R.H.A. Group
    on 105-104-143 and on 106-108-113.

(c) 22 F.A. Bde
    2 Batteries on TRIVELET
    1 Battery on 125.

The above batteries will also begin firing (but at a moderate rate of fire) at 9.50 a.m. and continue till further orders except that the R.H.A. batteries firing on 105-104-143 will stop firing on the length 105-104 at 10.40 a.m. but continue to fire ~~from the road elbows~~ along that trench from the 1st of the road elbows by MOULIN DE PIETRE up to 143.

(7) Both the R.H.A. group (14th H.A. Bde.) and the 35th F.A. Bde, at head quarters XX Inf. Bde (will have an officer)

(8) Captain R.W. Lamb. R.A. (F.O.O. at M.23.D.4.6) will report at 7. a.m. as to weather conditions, regarding probability of being able to observe fire at 7.30 a.m. His report will be telephoned to 7th D.A. as quickly as possible.

(9) In the event of it being reported that the morning is too misty for proper observation of fire at 7.30 a.m., the bombardment and subsequent attack will be postponed until such time as the weather betters

9. Cont

~~In such case the attack will begin 30 minutes preceding after the hour fixed for time of commencement of the bombardment which will be notified to all concerned.~~ Cancelled

⑩ OC. 35 ?.A. Bde is arranging to communicate with HQS. 7th Div Arty by tapping into the cable of T battery representative with 20 Inf Bde HQS.

SWRawlins
Maj. RA.
Brigade Major. 7th D.A.

12/3/15.

Issued at ~~7.30~~ 6.30 am.

Copies to 7th Div
XX Inf Bde.
R.H.A. Group
22 ?.A. Bde
35. ?.A. Bde
7th Seige Group.

Appendix **VI**

Instructions for **VII** Divisional & Attached Artillery
~~and the infantry~~ for 12th March 1915.

1. Our infantry hold the line 1 - 2 - 90 - 89 up towards 86 approximately.

2. Two Bat^ns **XX**^th Inf. B^de are to attack the area road elbow by MOULIN DE PIETRE - 103 - 102 - 101 - 100 - 99 - big House N.W. of 102 - 105 - 104.

3. The attack will be preceded by 40 mins. bombardment which will begin at 9.50 a.m.

6. In addition to those batteries actually bombarding the area of attack, the remaining artillery will assist the attack by their fire as follows:—

(b) R.H.A. Group.
 on 105 - 104 - 143 and on 106 - 108 - 113

App VII

MESSAGES AND SIGNALS.

Army Form C. 2121.

TO: R.H.A. Group
22nd & 35th F.A. Bdes
7th Siege Group.

APPENDIX VII

Sender's Number: BM 50   **Day of Month:** 13th   AAA

Ref. 1/40,000 & 1/10000 maps.

1. Our new line (approximate) rests its left on our old trenches about M.29.b.4.8 and runs through M.29.b.10.0 to M.30.c.3.6. whence 8th Div. carries on the line towards M.36.a.10.3.

2. For the present the line will be held defensively as regards an immediate advance but local offensive action is to be energetically carried out.

3. 20th Inf. Bde. will from midnight to-night hold our new trenches, the 22nd Inf. Bde. holding the original trenches. The junction between Inf. Bdes. will be 100 yds West of the PIETRE road.

4. The 35th F.A. Bde. will cover the front of 20th Inf. Bde. and will detail an officer to represent them at Hd. Qrs. 20th Inf. Bde. This officer to be in telephonic communication with Hd. Qrs. 35th F.A. Bde.

5. R.H.A. Group will cover the front of 22nd Inf. Bde from the PIETRE road to the TRIVELET road.

6. 22nd F.A. Bde. will cover the front of 22nd Inf. Bde from the TRIVELET road (exclusive) to ROUGES BANCS. OC 22nd F.A. Bde. will maintain telephonic communication with Hd. Qrs. 22nd Inf. Bde.

7. OC R.H.A. Group (who is in telephonic communication with both 35th + 22nd F.A. Bdes) will be prepared to afford support at once on request on the fronts covered by the 35th + 22nd F.A. Bdes.

8. Os.C. R.H.A. Group and 22nd F.A. Bdes. will arrange for communication between F.O.O.s and Bn. Commanders in such cases as they consider to be necessary.

9. 7th Siege group will be at disposal of B.G.C.R.A.

From: 7th Div Arty
Time: 10.15 pm.

S.W.H. Lawhuis Major R.A.
Bm. 7. D.A.

"C" Form (Duplicate). Army Form C. 2121.
MESSAGES AND SIGNALS.

APPENDIX VII

TO: A & O U

Sender's Number	Day of Month	In reply to Number	
	14		AAA

It is essential to protect our troops today against counter attack AAA It is most important that hostile Arty. fireing on our front line of troops should be kept down AAA Special efforts must be made to discover and spot the direction from which any such fire is coming and to engage hostile guns concerned at once AAA It is not safe to turn fire S.W. or W of the M IN DU PIETRE road M 3 0 A and M 30 C.

Through A & O U

FROM: H.A. Groups
PLACE & TIME: 10.20 AM Arras

"C" Form (Duplicate). Army Form C. 2123.
MESSAGES AND SIGNALS.

TO: A Q V and 14th Bde R.H.A

Day of Month: 14

If our trenches are Bombarded Btys. will fire as follows:—

A on enemys guns N 32 C 32
Q "   "   "   N 31 C 95
V "   "   "   N 26 A 31
(14th R.H.A Bde   N 32 A 23)

If enemy bombards our trenches some guns must be at once turned on to his trenches opposite that part of ours which he is bombarding by that Bde. which covers the front in question —

FROM: H.A. Group
PLACE & TIME: 11.30 A.M.

Appendix VII

To   R.H.A Group.   22nd & 35th F.A. Bdes.
        7th Siege Group.

B.M. 50   13.3.15.

Ref 1/40,000 & 1/10,000 maps.

1. Our new line (approx.) rests its left on our old trenches about M.29.b.4.8. and runs through M.29.b.10.0. to M.30.c.3.6. whence 8th Div. carries on the line towards M.36.a.10.8?

2. For the present the line will be held defensively as regards an immediate advance, but local offensive action is to be energetically carried out.

5. R.H.A Group will cover the front of 22nd Inf. Bde. from the PIETRE road to the TRIVELET Road.

7. O.C. R.H.A. Group (who is in cmd. with both 35th & 22nd F.A. Bdes.) will be prepared to afford support at once on request on the fronts covered by the 35th & 22nd F.A. Bdes.

8. O's.C. R.H.A. Group & 22nd & F.A. Bdes will arrange for cmn. between F.O.O's and Bn. Cmdrs, in such cases as they consider to be necessary.

7th Div. Arty.   10.15. p.m.

Appendix VII

To R.H.A Group.   22nd & 35th F.A. Bdes.
    7th Siege Group.

B.M. 50   13.3.15.

Ref 1/40,000 & 1/10,000 maps.

1. Our new line (approx) rests its left on our old trenches about M.29.b.4.8. and runs through M.29.b.10.0. to M.30.c.3.6. whence 8th Div: carries on the line towards M.36.a.10.8?

2. For the present the line will be held defensively as regards an immediate advance, but local offensive action is to be energetically carried out.

5. R.H.A. Group will cover the front of 22nd Inf. Bde. from the PIETRE road to the TRIVELET Road.

7. OC. R.H.A. Group (who is in cme. with both 35th & 22nd F.A. Bdes) will be prepared to afford support at once on request on the fronts covered by the 35th & 22nd. F.A. Bdes.

8. O's.C. R.H.A. Group & 22nd & F.A. Bdes will arrange for cme. between F.O.Os and Bn. Cmdrs, in such cases as they consider to be necessary.

7th Div. Arty.   10.15. pm.

Appendix VII

To A. Q & U

14th.

It is essential to protect our troops today against counter attack AAA. It is most important that hostile Arty firing on our front line of troops should be kept down AAA. Special efforts must be made to discover and report the direction from which any such fire is coming and to engage hostile guns concerned at once AAA. It is not safe to turn fire S.W. or W. of the MOULIN DE PIETRE road M.30 A & M 30. C

H.A. Group.   10.20 am.

To A. Q. U. & 14th Bde R.H.A.

14th

If our trenches are bombarded batteries will fire as follows :-

    A on enemy's guns   N 32 C 32
    Q   "   "   "   N 31 C q 5
    U   "   "   "   N 26 A 31
    14th Bde R.H.A. ...   N. 32 A 23

If enemy bombards our trenches some guns must be at once turned onto his trenches opposite that part of ours which he is bombarding, by that bde. which covers the front in question

H. A. Group.

11. 30 AM.

App VIII

MESSAGES AND SIGNALS.

"A" Form. Army Form C. 2121. No. of Message

Office of Origin and Service Instructions.

Ref 1/1 v 000 map

This message is on a/c of:
SECRET Service
APPENDIX VIII
(Signature of "Franking Officer.")

TO { RHA Group
~~22nd F.A. Bde.~~ ~~7th Siege Group~~
~~35th F.A. Bde.~~ }

Sender's Number: BM 57
Day of Month: 14th
AAA

1. During the night 14th/15th the 8th Division takes over the whole of the newly acquired front line from its junction with the Indian Corps up to but exclusive of "E" and "F" lines. "E" and "F" lines are to be held by one Brigade (22nd) of the 7th Division.

This re-arrangement is to be completed by 6 am to-morrow.

2. Artillery Zones are reallotted as follows:—

(a). 35th FA Bde.

From our right to the FAUQUISSART–TRIVELET road.

The 35th FA Bde will be prepared to afford immediate support on the front of the trenches to be taken over from us by 8th Div. and to that end will establish telephonic communication with the nearest artillery brigade of 8th Div.

(b). R.H.A. Group

The FAUQUISSART–TRIVELET road (exclusive) to the line 132–133.

"A" Form.   Army Form C. 2121.

MESSAGES AND SIGNALS.   No. of Message

Prefix	Code	m.	Words	Charge	This message is on a/c of:	Recd. at	m.
Office of Origin and Service Instructions.			Sent			Date	
			At	m.	Service.	From	(2
			To			By	
			By		(Signature of "Franking Officer.")		

TO

| * | Sender's Number | Day of Month | In reply to Number | AAA |

(C). 22nd F.A. Bde.

The line 132 — 133 (exclusive) to our left.
This Bde. will be prepared to afford immediate support to the right of the Canadian Division, with the nearest artillery brigade of which it is in communication through 14th H.A. Bde.

3. The 22nd F.A. Bde. is in telephonic communication with Hd. Qrs. 22nd Inf. Bde. and will be the medium of conveyance of requests for fire &c from B.G.C. 22nd Inf. Bde. to other Artillery Brigades.

4. Os.C. Brigades ~~with reserves~~ and R.H.A. Group will ensure that at least one officer is in direct communication with the infantry whose front they cover, by night if not also by day.

5. 7th Siege Group will continue to act under the direct orders of the B.G.C.R.A.

From   7th Div Arty
Place
Time   11 pm.

The above may be forwarded as now corrected.   (Z)

Censor.   Sutton Jenkins Major R.A.
Signature of Addressee or person authorised to telegraph in his name

* This line should be erased if not required.   BM 7 DG

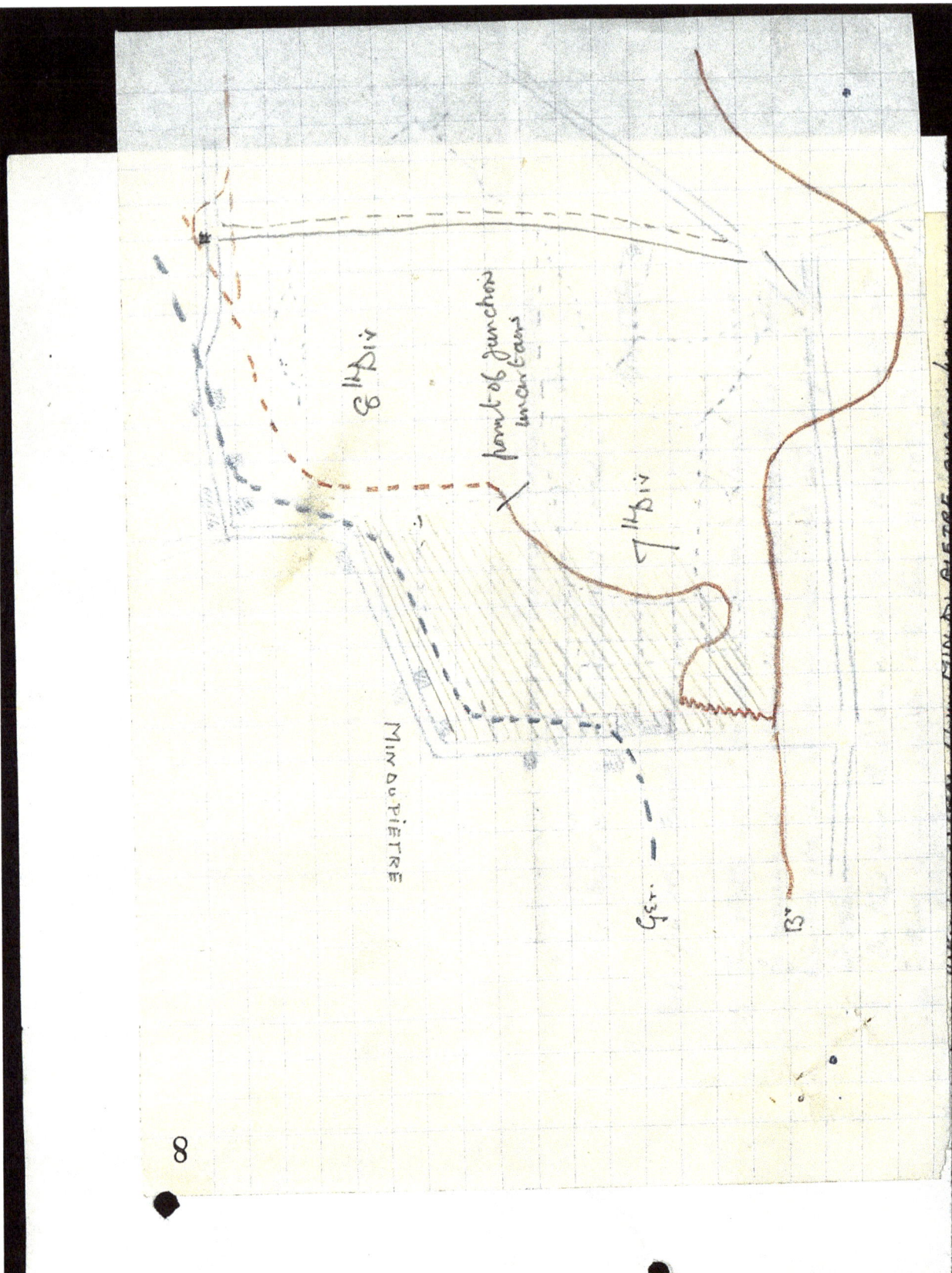

Information on area between communication trenches ①—88 and ②—100 and the MIN DU PIETRE — BACQUEROT road.

BM 58A

Ref. 1/10,000 French map.

1. The whole area (shaded) is rendered almost impassable by innumerable trenches, ditches and large holes. These trenches etc are in many cases broad and deep and full of water.

2. In this area there are many small ridges mounds and
※ hollows running parallel to the line 102–103. These obscure rifle fire to the N. Near M in MIN DU PIETRE enemy have machine guns well concealed West of the houses at the Elbow but not inside the houses.

3. 86 + 88 is another strongly defended locality. A thick wood runs behind this road in the direction 86–104 as far as the Elbow. The houses along the road still offer cover for infantry when not actually under fire.

4. The new front line is shown on accompanying sketch.

5. It is considered that it would be hazardous for us to attempt to put shell anywhere within the area mentioned in paras 1 & 2, & not to be attempted without most careful & constant observation.

14.3.15

※ These hollows do not obscure fire to S or S.E. in which directions field of fire is good.

"A" Form.   Army Form C. 2121.

MESSAGES AND SIGNALS.   No. of Message

Prefix	Code	m.	Words	Charge	This message is on a/c of:	Recd. at	m.
Office of Origin and Service Instructions.			Sent			Date	
			At	m.	Service.	From	
			To				
			By		(Signature of "Franking Officer.")	By	

TO { Ha Corp
22ⁿᵈ H.A. Bde   7ᵗʰ Siege Corp
35ᵗʰ H.A. Bde

Sender's Number	Day of Month	In reply to Number	AAA
BM 55	14ᵗʰ		

Ref BM 54 following additional information to hand
Legris enemy have about 6 Bns on front LE
MAISNIL — PIETRE and about ten thousand men on
front PIETRE — RICHEBOURG L AVOUE aaa artillery
of 6ᵗʰ Bavarian Reserve Regiment arrived about
2 pm yesterday aaa Germans have standing orders to
recapture any lost Trenches at all costs aaa
enemy losses estimated at 2000 prisoners 4000
killed 12000 wounded

From	7	D. A.		
Place				
Time	2 pm.			

The above may be forwarded as now corrected.   (Z)

Censor.   Signature of Addressor or person authorised to telegraph in his name

Bm 7 D.A

"A" Form. Army Form C. 2121.

MESSAGES AND SIGNALS.   No. of Message ____

Prefix ____ Code ____ m.	Words	Charge	This message is on a/c of:	Recd. at ____ m.
Office of Origin and Service Instructions.	Sent			Date ____
	At ____ m.		Service.	From ____
	To			By ____
	By		(Signature of "Franking Officer.")	

TO { H.Q. Group.
      22nd F.A. Bde.
      35th F.A. Bde.

| Sender's Number | Day of Month | In reply to Number | AAA |
| BM 68 | 16th | | |

1. 35th F.A. Bde. will take over at once the support of the left Bn. of the left Brigade (Bde. H.Q. at M.23.a.8.0.) from and including to-night. This Bde. will maintain an officer with Hd. Qrs. 24th (to-night relieved by 23rd) Inf. Bde. and another with the Bn. which holds the front point 99 (1/10000 French map) to CHAPIGNY.

2. The RHA Group will consequently extend its responsibilities to its right, and now cover the front of 22nd Inf. Bde. (7th Div.) from CHAPIGNY to the line 132 - 133. ~~until further~~ OC RHA Group will replace with his own officers such officers as the 35th F.A. Bde. has had with the infantry in the 35th Bde. front hitherto.

3. 22nd F.A. Bde. remains as before.
4. B.G.C. 22nd Inf. Bde. informed. acknowledged by telephone

From	7th Div. Arty.
Place	
Time	4.15 pm.

The above may be forwarded as now corrected. (Z)   S.W. Rawlins Major RA

Censor. Signature of Addresser or person authorized to telegraph in his name

* This line should be erased if not required.

BM JDG

INTELLIGENCE. G 443.

The following information on NEUVE CHAPELLE and its vicinity has been collected from late residents of the village and from various reconnaissances.

I. The Village.

1. Most of the houses in the village have been strongly built of brick and contain cellars; only a small proportion of the houses are built of light material such as lath and plaster.

The buildings marked (a) (b) (c) (d) (e) (f) (g) are the principal ones of those strongly built and, though perhaps considerably knocked about, should still be capable of affording strong defensive localities.

The following is a short description of each—

(a) A chateau surrounded by meadow land with a few trees near the house. The south western boundary consists of a very thick high hedge, while at the S.W. corner near the road are two high parallel brick walls which, before the war, were used as a miniature range. The road front has a low brick wall with iron railings.

(b) A strong brick building with a strip of thick undergrowth along the northern edge not far from the house. No walls existed here but it is believed that a rubble and sandbag parapet has been built along the north and south sides outside the building: a house used to exist at the point of the angle made by the two roads, but it is now in ruins.

(c) A strong brick building surrounded by a brick wall.

(d) A high house overlooking the orchard to the west, the upper part being built of lath and plaster.

(e) A large brewery, substantially built with numerous large cellars. The building to the north on the opposite side of the road is a large corrugated iron roofed shed and is surrounded on 3 sides by a brick wall 3 foot high.

(f) A strongly built house at the eastern edge of the village "Place" which is immediately south of the church (57). To the S.W. of the house is a garden (h) enclosed by a strong brick wall.

(g) A strongly built house surrounded by a brick wall.

2. The church (57) is surrounded on 3 sides by a cemetery; on the fourth or northern side is a garden (j), separated from the church by a ditch, and on a higher level than the road running along its northern edge.

3. North of the above road and the church is a large closely planted orchard (32) with a smaller thinly planted orchard and vegetable garden (k) beyond it; along the northern and western edges of both these orchards are tall poplars. The western edge of orchard (32) is reported to be a small thicket (n) of dense undergrowth, while at the S.E. edge is a large meadow (l) divided from the orchard by a large wide ditch.

4.

4.   The area south of the church between (38) and (63) is very enclosed and consists of small meadows and gardens with thick hedges, many of which are reported to be wired.

5.   The road west of the village and north (and east) of (62) does not exist.

II. Area west of NEUVE CHAPELLE.

1.   West of the orchard (32) and within the area (62) (43) (39) (69) are two large meadows. Their western boundary is a very thick hedge (p) and along the southern boundary runs a row of large trees including some oaks.

2.   At (43) is a small house, reported not to be very strongly built and near (42) are the ruins of a burnt farm. At (27) is a solid brick farm which has been partially burnt.

3.   The line (43) (40) (17) is a footpath with a wide ditch on the western side; between (42) and (40) it is sunken and some 5 ft. below the ground on either side.

III. Area north of NEUVE CHAPELLE.

1.   The buildings at (48) are strongly built of brick, between these buildings and the road at (50) to the east, is a thickly planted orchard.

The buildings at cross roads (18) are newly and very strongly built: the two meadows to the south of it and on either side of the road, between (22) and (47), have very thick and strong hedges on their western boundaries. At (17½) is a ruined farm. At (19) is a small farm partly built of brick, standing in a large open meadow, along the northern boundary of which runs a ditch (54) (52) (78) which is 6 ft. wide.

At (22) is a small house with an orchard.

2.   Further to the north lies a closely planted orchard (6) with a ditch surrounding it, and a strongly built brick farm close to the road. West of this farm and road on which it stands and towards (77) lies a large meadow with a row of tall trees round its borders. The road, where it passes between orchard (6) and this meadow, is at a somewhat lower level than either of them.

East of the orchard (6) the ditch which runs from (23) towards (4) is 10 ft. wide, and deep and always carries water.

IV.

IV Area N.E. and East of NEUVE CHAPELLE.

1.   The houses along the road (51) (98) are mostly of lath and plaster except the two farms at ( ) which are of (93) brick. The house (m) is a high brick building and somewhat overlooks the country to the S.W.

2.   The ground between the BOIS DE BIEZ and NEUVE CHAPELLE is bare and open; the RIVIERE DES LAYES is reported to be a ditch 3 ft. deep and 4 yards wide and very muddy at this time of year on both banks. At ( ) the banks are steep. The ground on both sides of the river from the BOIS DE BIEZ and NEUVE CHAPELLE slopes gradually towards it.

3.   The houses on the road running along the west of the BOIS DE BIEZ are small cottages with small gardens, very few being strongly built. The western edge of the BOIS DE BIEZ does not come up to the road as is shown on some maps.

4.   The country between NEUVE CHAPELLE - BOIS DE BIEZ and the MIN DU PIETRE - Ht. POMMERAU road is bare and open and affords little cover except in the water cuts and ditches.

Special Order.

To the 1st Army.

We are about to engage the enemy under very favourable conditions. Until now in the present campaign, the British Army has, by its pluck and determination, gained victories against an enemy greatly superior both in men and guns. Reinforcements have made us stronger than the enemy in our front. Our guns are now both more numerous than the enemy's are, and also larger than any hitherto used by any army in the field. Our Flying Corps has driven the Germans from the air.

On the Eastern Front, and to South of us, our Allies have made marked progress and caused enormous losses to the Germans, who are, moreover, harassed by internal troubles and shortage of supplies, so that there is little prospect at present of big reinforcements being sent against us here.

In front of us we have only one German Corps, spread out on a front as large as that occupied by the whole of our Army (the First).

We are now about to attack with about 48 battalions a locality in that front which is held by some three German battalions. It seems probable, also, that for the first day of the operations the Germans will not have more than four battalions available as reinforcements for the counter attack. Quickness of movement is therefore of first importance to enable us to forestall the enemy and thereby gain success without severe loss.

At no time in this war has there been a more favourable moment for us, and I feel confident of success. The extent of that success must depend on the rapidity and determination with which we advance.

Although fighting in France, let us remember that we are fighting to preserve the British Empire and to protect our homes against the organized savagery of the German Army. To ensure success, each one of us must play his part, and fight like men for the Honour of Old England.

(Sd.) D. HAIG, General,
Commanding 1st Army.

9th March, 1915.

1st Printing Co., R.E.   G.H.Q   573.

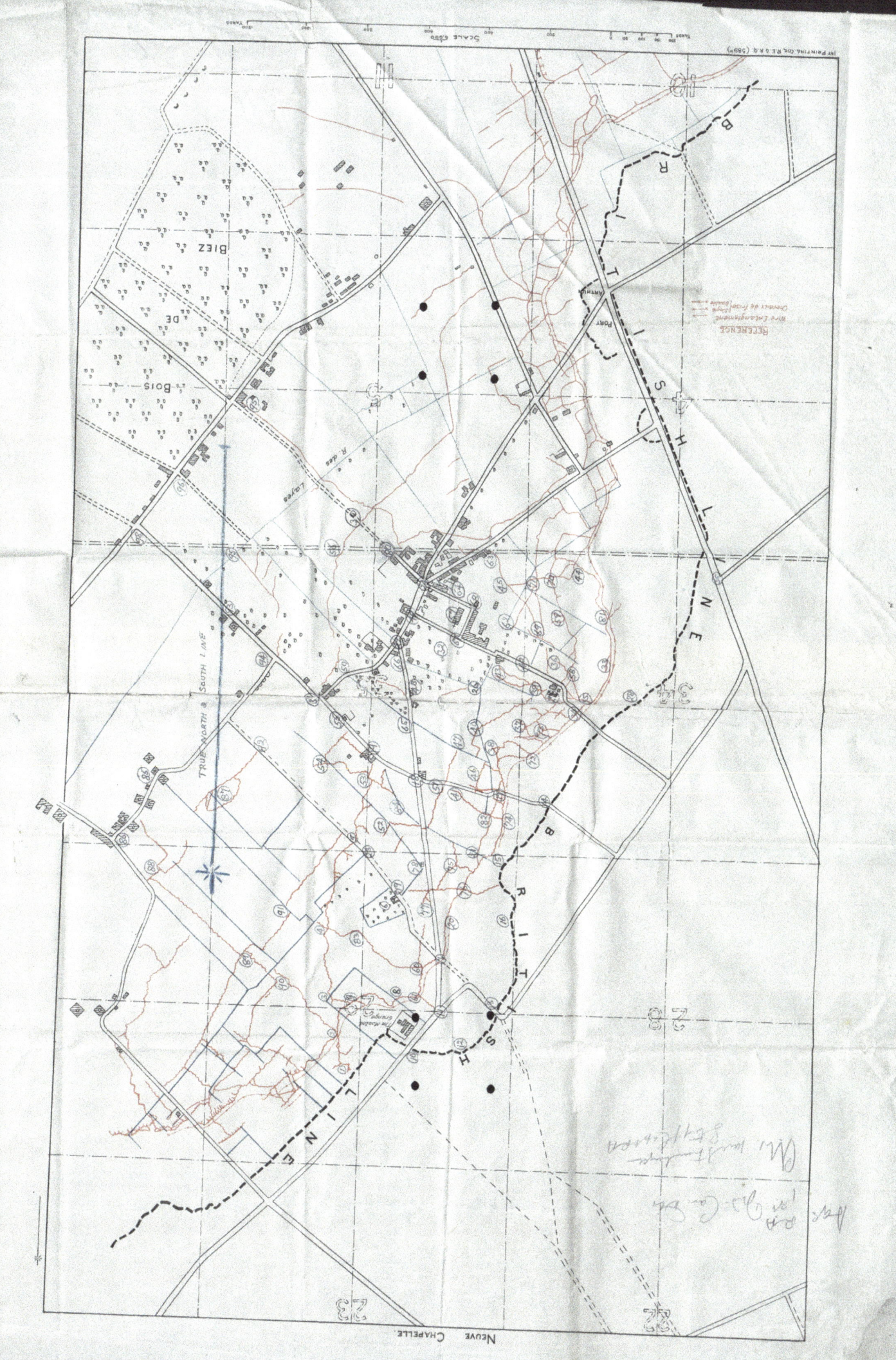

Dr R A
3 Cap" Ann Chapin
Marblehead

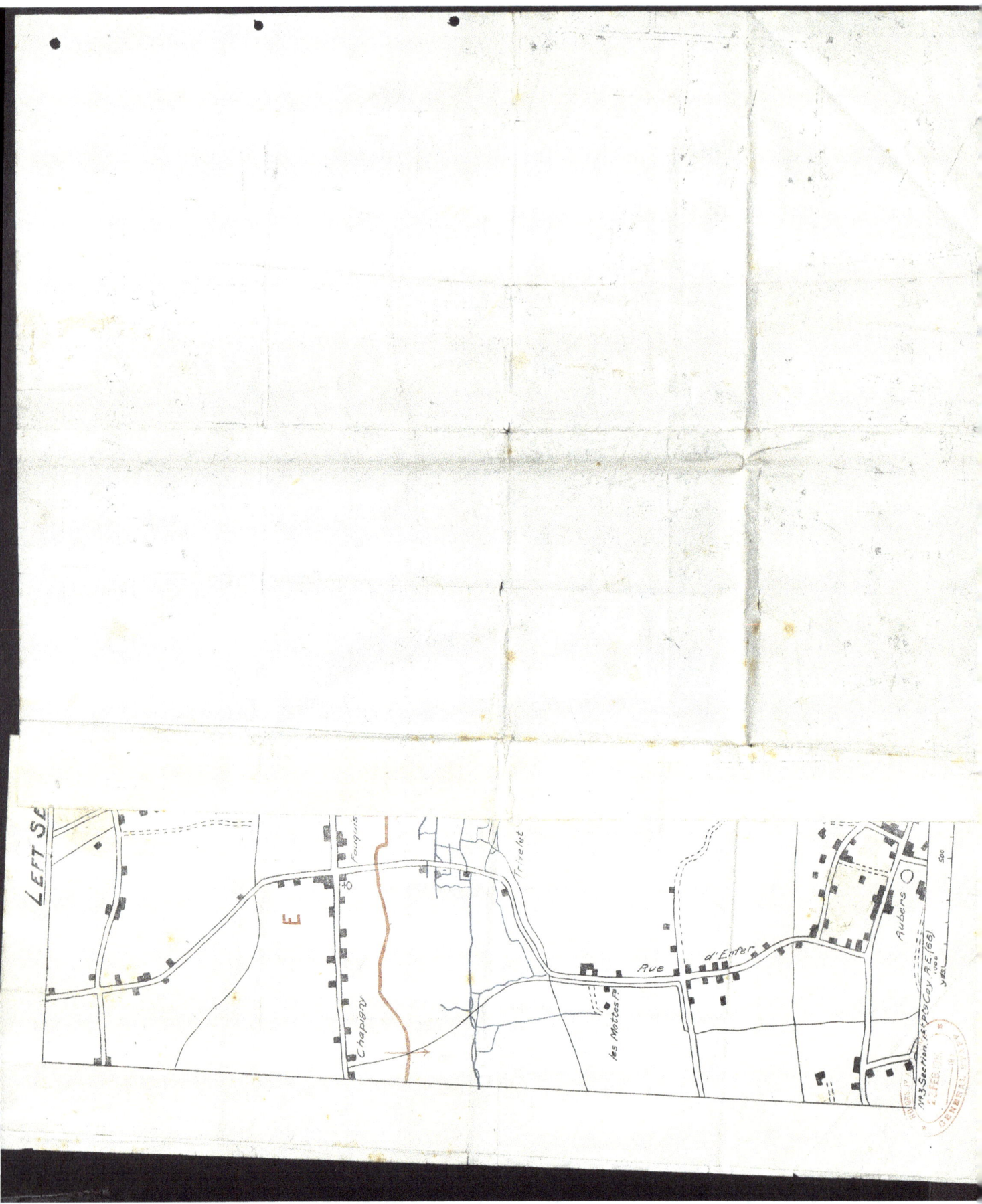

LEFT SECTION 8TH DIVISION.

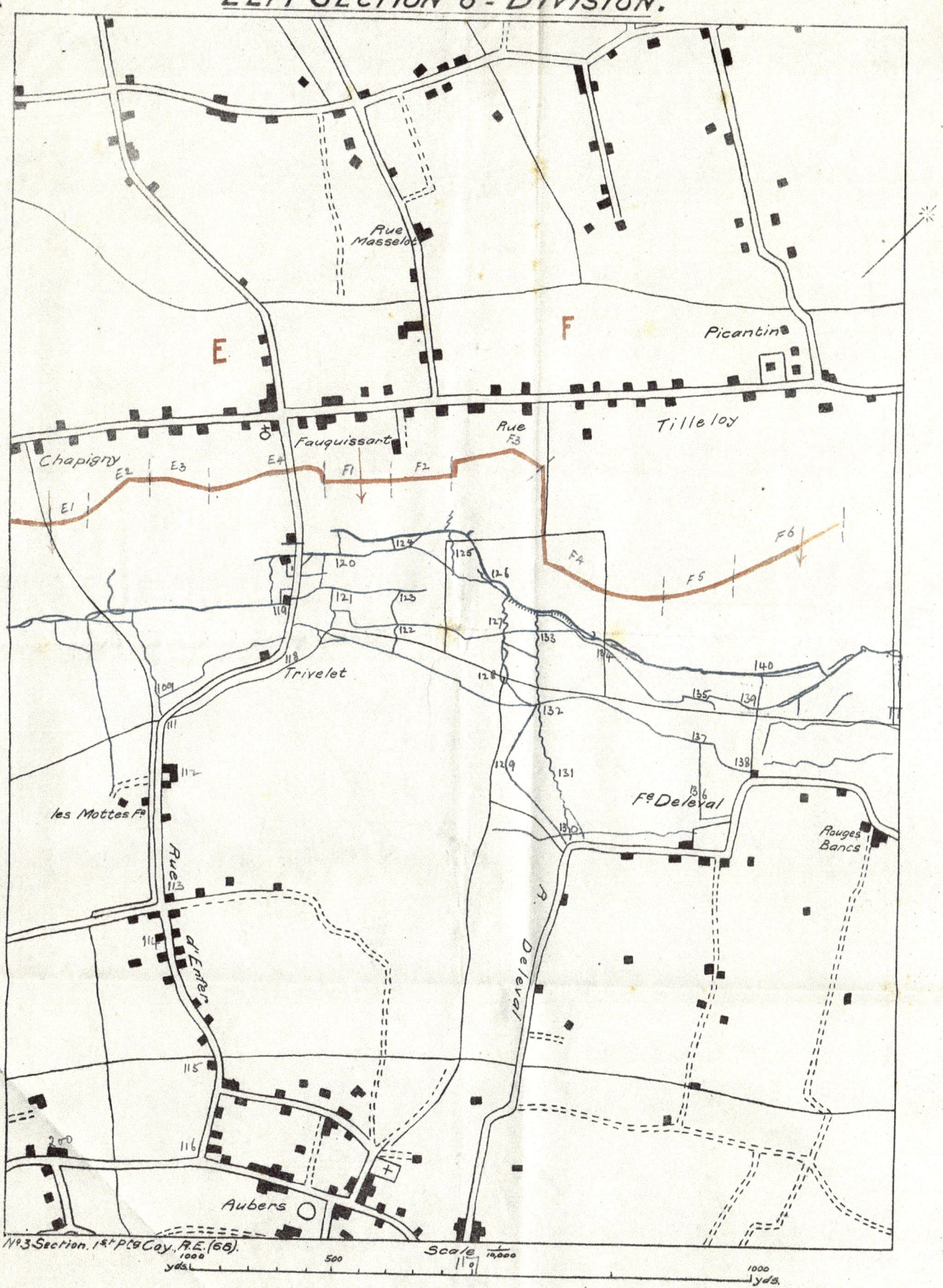

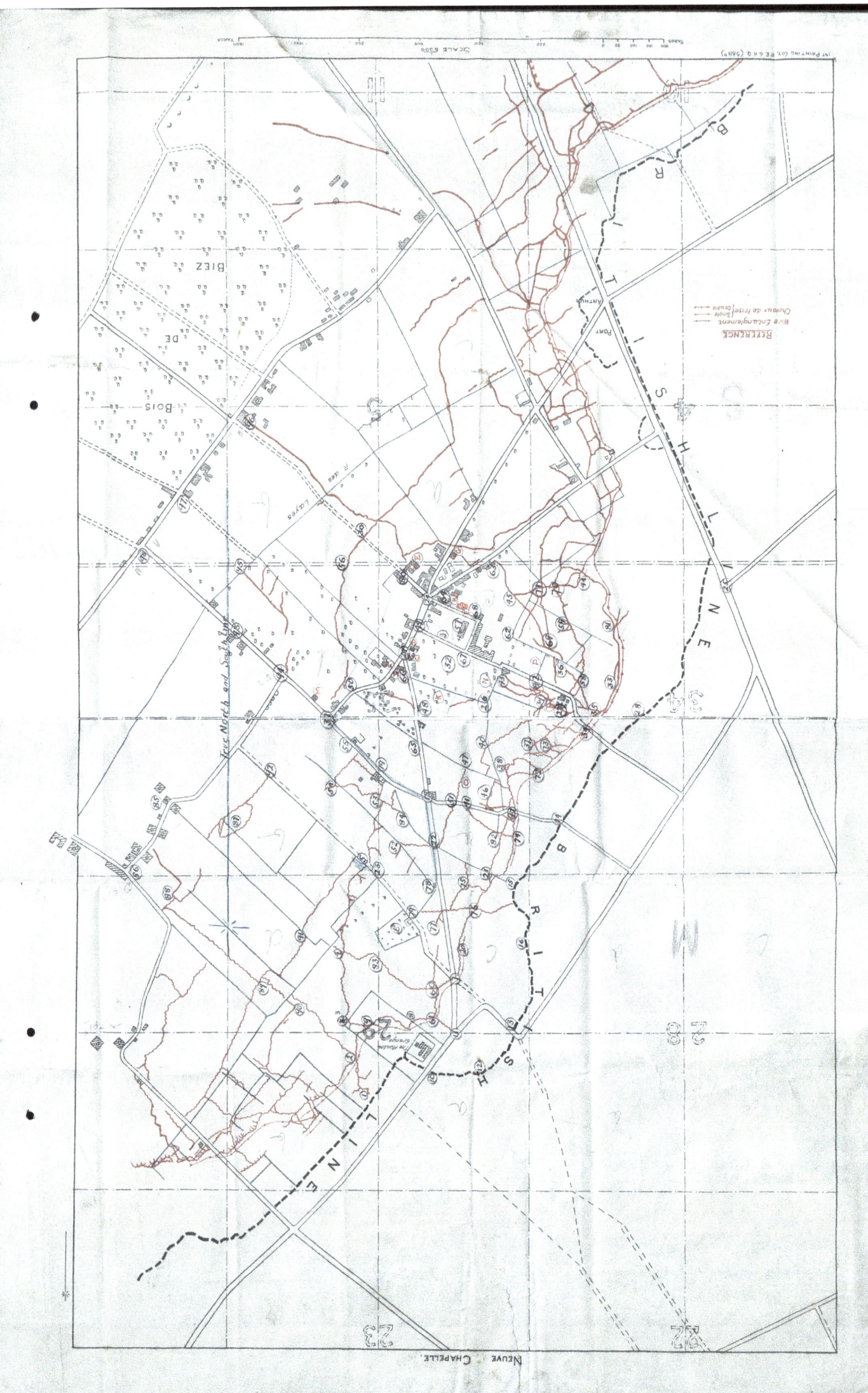

Serial No 49.

121/5799

With Appendices.

WAR DIARY

OF

Head Quarters R.A. 1st Indian Cavalry Division.

From 7th April 1915 to 28th May 1915.

WAR DIARY HQS. R.A. 1st IND. CAV. DIV.   Army Form C. 2118.

INTELLIGENCE SUMMARY.

(Erase heading not required.)

Instructions regarding War Diaries and Intelligence Summaries are contained in F.S. Regs., Part II, and the Staff Manual respectively. Title pages will be prepared in manuscript.

A.G's OFFICE AT THE BASE
No. 94b.N.3
5 JUN. 1915
INDIAN SECTION

Hour, Date, Place.	Summary of Events and Information.	Remarks and references to Appendices.
RUE DE PARADIS LAVENTIE APRIL 7th		last APPENDIX VIII
APRIL 16th 17th	Orders received from 7th Div. Arty. that 2 btys. could be noted leaving our bty. in action. A and U Btys. moved from their positions during the 17th – 8th to billets N. of Paras LYS – Q Bty. remained in action covering right front of O.C. 35th Bde R.F.A. who is now responsible for support of Right half of 7th Div. Trenches – Divnl. Amn. Cm. brought up to establish amnt. shown in pages 72-4 War Estb. Exped. Force. – Drivers were not available accordingly gunners were sent up, experiment planned & ordered. Motive power used until more British gunners in forward in riding during – U Bty. reoccupied old gun position at LA FLINQUE. Q Bty. marched back to billets vacated by U Bty. Front the C.R.H.A. was called to a conference at 3rd D.A. H.Q.S. SAILLY Where plans were formed. A WW Rty. would in the near future be employed attached to temporarily to FLEURBAIX.	MAP 36 N.W.3 EDITION
19th	HQS RHA CO and A & Q Btys. marched to billets at LA CROIX to-BARRETS and Pores to H.Q'S. – Bty. position extending along RUE DES BOMBARD Commanded the Jug. HQ'S. moved to billet at LA CROIX LES CORNEX. – One Section U Bty. marched to Irajon line billets H21A & after 8 pm on section proceed Relieving in a 4 mg front action. –	
20	Div. Amtn. Cm. marched to billets H.S.A.B. – One established from Retra. H.Q. to 5 Rgt. Rt. A. 9th D.A. & wingwich section Q A.C.v.	
FLEURBAIX 21st		

Army Form C. 2118.

15

WAR DIARY
HQrs. R.H.A. 1st IND. CAV. DIV.
or INTELLIGENCE SUMMARY.
(Erase heading not required.)

Instructions regarding War Diaries and Intelligence Summaries are contained in F. S. Regs., Part II, and the Staff Manual respectively. Title pages will be prepared in manuscript.

Hour, Date, Place.	Summary of Events and Information.	Remarks and references to Appendices. Last APPENDIX VII
LA CROIX LESCORNE & FLEURBAIX 22nd APRIL 23rd	Registration continued each Bty from 3.6.p.m. Q.B.9 had one casualty (killed). Registration continued - the Germans also registering, but not on our gun pits.	
24th	All 3 Btys registered in morning - burst was received at 4.30 p.m. that 4 guns March Bty were to be prepared to march - one section presently to take Lutrythuck under orders of O.C. 5th Rista Bde at 6 p.m. who kisinel for Rtys Ismard, and alone together with 2 section 4 Div. Artry C.M. to ST MARIE CAPPEL - marched at 8 p.m. via ESTAIRES. NEUFBERQUIN STRAZEELE road - Battery Staff Officer of 13 Ind. Cav. Div. marched road at Billet in arrived ST SYLVESTRE - Btys. arrived about 2 a.m. 25. Tired billets within 14 Ind. Cav. Div. area	By G.R.O. we are now called the 1st / INDIAN R.H.A. BRIGADE
25th	R.H.A. HQs. at HANGMAR HOUCK Chateau Stop in Wills command between that and ST MARIE CAPPEL.	
26th & 27th	Remained ready to move at short notice.	
28th	Recd. orders at 12 that Division would move at 12.45 to march WATAU - R.H.A. following SIALKOT CAV. BDE. Into billets about AU THULYS. Otrys being together in a gun field.	
29-30th	Remained ready to move at short notice. Pleasful.	
1st May	Division from YPRES - of refugees from YPRES - 1st May Divisn recd. at 11 p.m. to march back at 6 a.m. tomorrow.	O.W. van Stranbyle Capt. + Adjt. 1st Ind. R.H.A. Bde

WAR DIARY

1st INDIAN Cav. R.H.A. BRIGADE

INTELLIGENCE SUMMARY.

(Erase heading not required.)

Army Form C. 2118.

Hour, Date, Place.	Summary of Events and Information.	Remarks and references to Appendices.
NATAU 25th Mar 6 A.M.	The DIVISION marched back to billets at GASSEL following AMBALA & LUCKNOW Cav. Bde. — At 4.30 p.m. received prov. Cav. Corps Orders for the Bde. to march via HAZEBROUCK and MERVILLE to report to 1st ARMY. Adv. M. ahead in car to obtain from 8th DIV. ARTY. details of billets near N of RIVER LYS. (G 8 and 9).	LAST APPENDIX VIII
3rd 2 A.M.	Btys. & Cav. marched into billets N of River Lys.	MAP 36
FLEURBAIX 4.30 p.m.	Btys. moved to recupr. Red posns in Rue LOMBARD commencing 7.30 p.m. — Wagon lines H 2 d —	
4th	Btys. moved tactical previous pt.	
7th 9-10	8th DIV OPERATION ORDER received together with VIII Div. Op. ORDER — APPENDIX 9 — Operation postponed 24 hrs. —	
5 A.M. 9th	Bombardment commenced in accordance with orders issued Tasks for Gp GROUP during the day Appendix 11 — also	and TIMETABLE OF TASKS APPENDIX 10.
	night line for 9-10th	Auth. Appendix
4 A.M. 15th	Bombardment ordered afterwards Cancelled. No movement	
	or other firing.	
12 noon	Preliminary orders for the general move tonight recd.	
2.30 p.m.	Confirm. and Op. Rote went out with Bde MAR 7 DA.	
8.45 p.m.	Bde. marched via FLEURBAIX — LAVENTIE — LA GORGUE — LESTREM — LOCON to GORRE — Advtn. Rev. Rty. occupied position in and near em- Bremont Hortouse night (1 A.M.) thereunder of & ammunition. As. 7th Div marched to

Army Form C. 2118.

17

WAR DIARY
1st IND. R.H.A. or BRIGADE
INTELLIGENCE SUMMARY.
(Erase heading not required.)

Instructions regarding War Diaries and Intelligence Summaries are contained in F. S. Regs., Part II, and the Staff Manual respectively. Title pages will be prepared in manuscript.

Hour, Date, Place.	Summary of Events and Information.	Remarks and references to Appendices.
GORRE. 11th	1st Div. area – Artillery croaked – Hqs. at Sailleen	LAST APPENDIX 11. Amn. expended: 12" noon–12 noon A – 76 Q – 63 U – 30
11th	Head of tunnel fork – B Section reported, front heavy and big sure tunnels	
Reference 1/10,000 12th	The enemy 4 pins pumps of 75's reopened points.	13 A – 114 Q – 57 U – 117
12th	June registering – Violent movements during night 6 to 8 pm to – Bombardment during night 8 rounds throughout the night.	14 A – 334 Q – 236 U – 371
VIEILLE-VIOLAINES.	Violent gunfire throughout the night. German counter-attack – Gun fire first 1 A.M. – 1.15 A.M. – German counter-attack – Heavy lights and artillery reprisal counter-attack. Appendix 12.	15th A – 195 Q – 187 U – 293
FESTUBERT. 14th	Orders issued for bombardment throughout the day. Appendix 13. 8.15 A.M. Appendix 13. Orders issued for bombardment commencing	APPENDIX 14
15th	Extracts from Div. Orders were attached together. Batt. – Instrs. FOR ARTILLERY – and ARTILLERY TIME TABLE.	A – 692 Q – 563 U – 943 From noon 15th to noon 16th
16th	2/Lieut M. HEATH CALDWELL killed. N Chestnut Troop killed, when reconnoitring for pt. for an advance Section about 6.10 A.M. – Section now forward about M3 – He went forward in command in rear in FESTUBERT. Forward about M3. Four horses were hit when they returned after dark so no sharp left attack (2"Div.) not having got points. Left flank been too exposed. A Section (Lt. DALE) "U" Sty. Rotated to opposite M3. Occupied position at 5pm. night 15th – Object before afternoon front line parapet. – was not fired on by German artillery. Only no casualties –	

Army Form C. 2118.

WAR DIARY

HQS 1ST IND. R.H.A. BDE.

INTELLIGENCE SUMMARY.

(Erase heading not required.)

Instructions regarding War Diaries and Intelligence Summaries are contained in F. S. Regs., Part II, and the Staff Manual respectively. Title pages will be prepared in manuscript.

18

Last appendix 14

Hour, Date, Place.	Summary of Events and Information.	Remarks and references to Appendices.
1½mls. W. of FESTUBERT	16. The Bde. was used generally to barrage fire, BC's having a free hand to engage targets which they could see – firing orders for during the day as on APPENDIX 15.(a)	
	17th Firing took place as shown on FIRING REPORT APPENDIX 15(b) 17th A-413 Q-716 V-796 Inf. attack progressed and positions were reconnoitered. BSC. Cmds. O.C's A & D Btys. about M3. Guns were not moved forward.	76th A-692 Q-563 V-943 17th A-413 Q-716 V-796 18th A-692 Q-464 V-417
	18th BSE. was for shr barrage fire on points shown in Army Report (APPENDIX 15 (c)) Enemy's Arty. became aggressive and BSE. turned onto the supported position of 3 enemy Btys. about 529.B. A & Q tried repeatedly and German Btys. stopped to reopen again about 4 hrs. – Infantry 122. BSE. asked for suppressive Btys. fire in their new positions from enemy's shrapnel fire –	
	19th Anti. Park experiencing great difficulty in getting filled all railways having been depleted – Btys. were down to answering great enemy – Ammo. front in evening still unsatisfactory and Ammn. Clmn. not completed from Park.	19th A-807 Q-563 V-240
	20th Same as yesterday – Gunn. Park both short & Btys. watchful hostilities in consequence – our target being enemy's Btys. – The Brigade has been in the F.O.O's. sending in information; and by night 17mn in Brick Communication with a Battalion HQS. – Canadian attacked at 8.45 pm – Btys. acted on B.M. 269 (APPENDIX 15(c))	20th A-44 Q-49 V-97

Army Form C. 2118.

WAR DIARY
or
INTELLIGENCE SUMMARY.
(Erase heading not required.)

LAST APPENDIX 15(c)

19

Hour, Date, Place.	Summary of Events and Information.	Remarks and references to Appendices.
21st	Column completed - Park Short - Nothing - Order received about 4 P.M. for a probable move tonight about 9.30 P.M. being relieved by Canadian Btys. - This cancelled later and 9.15 P.M. recvd to march without relief by Canadian — Btys. left amidst considerable firing — several shell falling near U Bty - Y Le Brigade marched complete in direction of 1ND CAV. DIV. getting down about AIRE & West a 4 hours. — Hqs - A Bty and Div. Ammn. Clm. — WITTES U Bty. — WEST ROCQUETOIRE Q Bty. — CAUCHIE D'ECQUES	} map 1/80,000 St OMER
26th 27th	Brigade arrived about 4 A.M. — Btys. still a an R.H.A. Bge. — Dispersed Stas the nearer Cavy. Bge. in case of a sudden move. — Orders received that 1st IND CAV. DIV. would move tomorrow. Btys marched with Cav. Bges.; Ammn. Clm. Hqs. and Divn. Troops — Division billeted in and round STAPLE	
28th	DIVISION marched to area round RUBROUCK - Arneketum (30) men from each Cav. regiment embussed overnight towards VLAMERTINGHE - R.H.A. billets as follows:- HQS. = RUBROUCK A = 1½ and N.E. of RUBROUCK Q Div. Ammn. Clm. —	

A.H. van Straubenzee
Capt. R.H.A
1st IND
Bge.

COPIES OF TELEPHONE MESSAGES.

To ROYAL ARTILLERY.

Q 495   date 4th. May.

4th. Corps wire begins All Ammunition Echelons should be filled up to establishment. 4 point 5 Howitzer Ammunition should be carried in the following proportion 60 per cent E 40 per cent C. But B rounds now in Echelons in excess of this proportion need not be returned. Shrapnel must however be drawn to complete echelons to their proper proportions ends.

From 8th. Division.

Headquarters, 8th. Division.

S.C. 951. date 4.5.15.

Following received from 4th. Corps begins The two special guns may dump 250 rounds shrapnel in all and 250 rounds H.E. in all. Other guns to dump as follows :-

     13 pr. 60 per gun.
     18 pr. 30 rounds shrapnel and
         10 H.E. per gun.
     4.5   20 rounds lyddite per gun.
     6"   60 Lyddite per gun.

We shall also have 7 % H.E. throughout all echelons for 18 prs. *will be drawn*

From 8th. Divl. Arty.

Officer Commanding,

     For information.

5.5.15.   Captain R.A.
              Staff Captain 8th. Div.Arty.

SUPPLY OF AMMUNITION

The following is the proposed scheme of supply of Ammunition to Brigade Ammunition Columns direct from Park. Reference attached sketch.

1. A central office will be established at Division Headquarters to which all requirements for ammunition by Brigade Ammunition Columns will be sent.

2. (a) The Columns of the following batteries marked Brown will be supplied along the Brown arrows. The empties returning by NOUVEAU MONDE and thence to SAILLY and across SAILLY BRIDGE.

   14th R.H.A. Brigade, 22nd R.F.A. Brigade, 7th Siege Brigade and 6th Siege Battery, 2nd WEST RIDING R.F.A. Brigade.

   (b) Columns marked Blue will be supplied by lorries moving along the Blue arrows. The 1st Indian R.H.A. Brigade lorries when empty, will return as shown in attached sketch and move across BAC ST MAUR BRIDGE.

   1st R.H.A. Brigade. 5th R.H.A. Brigade, 33rd R.F.A. Brigade.

   (c) Columns marked Red will be supplied by lorries moving along the Red arrows and these lorries when empty will return across SAILLY BRIDGE.

   35th R.F.A. Brigade. 37th R.F.A. Brigade. 45th R.F.A. Brigade.

   (d) The 3rd R.H.A. Brigade lorries will move, when empty, via BELLE CROIX and cross the river at PT LEVIS.

C.G. Stranach
Captain. R.A.
Staff Captain 8th Division Artillery.

5-5-15.

7.D.A. No: B.M.295.

1st H.A. Bde

According to latest information British troops hold the following line:-

K.5 - K.4 - L.2 whence a trench runs S.E. to our old line about A.2.a.8.8. Line runs on from L.2 to L.1 - Salient S.W. of M.3 - N.3 - M.5 - LA QUINQUE RUE road junction with a detached post at M.6. From LA QUINQUE RUE line runs on to P.11 - P.10 - a dug.out at present unoccupied trench runs on to Q.7 where there is a detached post.

The main line runs from Q.5 - half way between Q.3 and Q.2 to the saphead 200 yards due East of Q.2 - R.3 - R.5 - V.1. The Guards may have a post 150 yards due West of P.14.

It is still uncertain whether there are British Troops or not about M.9 M.10 M.12 M.4 L.7. It is thought that the area M.3 - M.4 - L.8 - L.6 - K.1 - L.3 is probably unoccupied by either British or Germans. Some British Troops were seen yesterday about M.4 or L.7, probably the latter, but no definite information is yet available as to this.

19th May, 1915.

Major, R.A.

List of Enemy Gun Positions within 6,000 yards, which have been located by Airmen within the last ten days; but it is not known which are and which are not occupied.

----*§*----

8 heavy guns	A.6.a.2.2.		S.30.c.8.9.		T.7.a.3.1.
Battery,,,,	M.36.c.7.3.		T.1.c.8.7.		T.7.c.3.9.
4.2" How'rs	S.6.b.5.5.	8 pits	T.2.a.7.5.		T.14.a.0.0.
	S.6.b.8.7.		T.7.c.9.8.	*	S.29.b.8.5.
	S.12.b.5.0.		T.8.a.3.5.	*	S.29.b.5.5.
1 gun......	S.12.c.6.8.		T.8.a.3.7.	*	S.29.b.2.3.
*	S.11.d.3.3.		T.13.a.6.7.		T.19.d.9.9.
*	S.29.a.9.5.		T.14.c.10.0		A.5.b.9.9.
*	S.29.d.6.2.		T.19.a.1.3.	4.2" Hows*§	S.28.b.5.0.
*	S.24.b.2.9.		T.19.c.4.8.		S.30.b.2.3.
*	S.24.b.0.10		T.19.c.9.4.		S.30.a.8.1.
	T.21.c.9.0.	8" Hows	T.21.c.5.4.		S.30.central
	S.30.b.4.3.		T.14.d.10.9		S.30.b.3.0.

§ (L.17)
* The most recent targets and most active.

7.D.A. No: B.M.S.63.

1st.
All Brigades RHA

1. In order to check the present excessive hostile artillery fire, zones are allotted to Brigades as follows:-

   35th Brigade R.F.A. – Squares A.3. 4. 5.
   French Batteries   – Squares A.3. 10. 11. 12. 13. 7.
   35th Brigade R.F.A.– Squares B.27. 23. 29.
   22nd Brigade R.F.A.– Squares B.22. 23. 24.

   Brigades will endeavour to locate and silence hostile artillery within their zones.

2. One battery per Brigade will observe their defensive zones and fire on enemy working parties, moving troops, etc., that may show themselves.

3. H.A. Brigades will be considered in hand but will fire on working parties, etc.

   Zones of observation:-
   14th Brigade R.H.A. – H.15 – RUE DU MARAIS.
   1st Brigade R.H.A. – RUE DU MARAIS to the South.

30th May, 1915.

Major, R.A.
Brigade Major, 7th Divisional Artillery.

COPY.   7D A. No: B.M. B.63.

1ST BRIGADE. R.H.A

1. In order to check the present excessive HOSTILE ARTILLERY FIRE, zones are allotted to BRIGADES as follows:-

   36TH BRIGADE R.F.A   SQUARES A 3. 4. 5.
   FRENCH BATTERIES.   SQUARES A 6. 10. 11. 12. 13. 7.
   35TH BRIGADE R.F.A.   SQUARES S 27. 28. 29
   22ND BRIGADE R.F.A   SQUARES S 22. 23. 24

   BRIGADES will endeavour to locate and silence HOSTILE ARTILLERY within their zones.

2. One BATTERY per BRIGADE will observe their defensive zones and fire on enemy working parties, moving troops etc., that may show themselves.

3. H.A BRIGADES will be considered in hand but will fire on working parties etc.
   Zones of observation:-
   14TH BRIGADE. R.H.A - M.15 - RUE DU MARAIS
   1ST BRIGADE R.H.A. RUE DU MARAIS to the SOUTH

20TH MAY. 1915.   MAJOR. R.A
                            BRIGADE MAJOR 7TH DIV. ARTY.

WAR DIARY

OF

1ST INDIAN R.H.A. BRIGADE

1ST INDIAN CAVALRY DIVISION

JUNE – DECEMBER – 1915

Serial N° 49.

WAR DIARY
OF
1st Indian R.H.A. Brigade

From 15th June 1915 to 30th June 1915.

Army Form C. 2118.

WAR DIARY
1st IND. R.H.A. or BDE.
INTELLIGENCE SUMMARY.
(Erase heading not required.)

Hour, Date, Place.	Summary of Events and Information.	Remarks and references to Appendices.
RUBROUCK 15th June	The Brigade accompanied the 1st Ind. Car. Bde. to trillula in area around ROQUETOIRE. Btys. marched with Cav. Bdes - Btys. billeted as follows - Hqs. - Chateau LAPREULE; A Bty. ECQUES; Q - REBECQUE; U - LIGNE; Div. Amn. Clm. LERENS	LAST APPENDIX 15(c)
35th June	Bde. still in rest billets - Btys. did training; with Stopping with Cav. Bde. Major Division arrangements - The best course to training we have yet had seen - Leave open to 3 P.M. Afternoon.	Aivound Stonehurst Capt. R.A. R.H.A. B.T.

Serial No. 49

121/1502

WAR DIARY
OF
1st Indian H.A. Brigade.

FROM — 1st July 1915 To 31st July 1915

Army Form C. 2118.

WAR DIARY
#1ST IND. R. of H.A. BDE.
INTELLIGENCE SUMMARY.
(Erase heading not required.)

Last appendix No. (15c)
H.R./100

21

Hour, Date, Place.	Summary of Events and Information.	Remarks and references to Appendices.
QUIESTEDE 1st July Chateau LAPREULE 15th July	Orders received that area was to be vacated for other troops and accordingly billets were allotted as follows:- Hqs. UPAN D'AVAL - 'A' Bty. LE WEMEL - "Q" - UPAN D'AVAL - "U" - NIELLES - Dn. Ammn. Cm. WESTREHAM. Later btys. were more concentrated under Col. ROUSE which necessitated the following changes:- Hqys. THEROUANNE - 'A' and 'Q' Bty & DELETTE - Training found suitable because	Reference 1/50,000 & 1/80,000 G.T. OTTER map.
15th July	practice.	
THEROUANNE BDE 29 July	Extracts from remarks of G.O.C. 1st Ind. Cav. Div. on the Report of O.C. A.S.C. on Dn. Ammn. Park in Inf. Cav. Divn. "G.O.C. Division is much gratified at his very fair report, but hopes he will furnish him a scale of his"	
31st July	Orders received that the Division will be [?] to move on 1st August.	

Alexander Rowley
Capt. & Adjt.
1st Ind. R.H.A. Bde.

Serial No 49.

12/6942

WAR DIARY
OF

Head Quarters 1st Indian R.H.A. Brigade.

From 1st August 1915 To 31st August 1915

Army Form C. 2118.

WAR DIARY

HQS. 1st IND. or R.H.A. BDE

INTELLIGENCE SUMMARY.

(Erase heading not required.)

22

Last appendix (15C)

Hour, Date, Place.	Summary of Events and Information.	Remarks and references to Appendices.
1915		
THEROUANNE 1st Aug.	The Bde. marched with its Btys. and sec. of Dn. Amn. Clm. attached to their Cavalry Bdes. The HQs. R.H.A. were attached Lucknow Bde. – RHA. marcha à deporte près hier. WESTREHEM – COYECQUE – FRUGES about 12 miles.	Map M04 1/80,000 – MATRINGHEM –
2nd	Bdehum visiting Ct Hqs. R.H.A. 'U' Bty. S.C. Anti. Clm., Field Squadron R.E., and 'A' Echelon Spares Imber Cl. Rouse marched via RUISSEAUVILLE – WAMBERCOURT – CAURON to ST VAAST. (20 ms) a wet day – marched large at night and took our horses might have in stable CHESDIN – transport couldn't utilise all along the road. Column marched via DOMPIERRE – NOYELLE.	
3rd	1 AM BUS – Start 9.30am, heavy rain – son in table Quellin. Bichel started at 6am. and was Dlarged 1½ hrs by a Supply Column – At 14 NOYELLE at 12.15 – on through YVRENCH to MAISON ROLAND will Hqs. R.H.A. were billeted – 25 mls.	
4th	Key been rain in morning. Shut march with Clubs en suite. Hqs. R.H.A. – LA HAIE (near SUR CAMP) 'A' Bty. – MOUFLERS 'Q' Bty. – Chateau VAUCHELLE 'U' Bty. – VAUCHELLE Dn. Ausn Clm. – SURCAMPS Dn. Pk. – SI RIQUIER = DOMART en PONTHIEU	

WAR DIARY
Hqs. 1st IND. R.H.A. B.DE.
INTELLIGENCE SUMMARY.

(Erase heading not required.)

Army Form C. 2118.

Hour, Date, Place.	Summary of Events and Information.	Remarks and references to Appendices.
Aug 1915		23 (4K)
LA HAIE SURCAMP		Last appendix (13c)
7th	Orders received for 2 Btys, and ammunition Br. Amm. Clm. to be ready to move tomorrow to join 5th D.A. & "X" Copl. "A" & "Q" Btys. warned —	
8th	"A" & "Q" each with 2/13 pr. 1st section of Br. Amm. Clm. marched to join 5th D.A.M. 1st Ech. truck halted at TREUX and one the under lieutenant. Fr 2 MAURICE R.F.A. 27th Bde. R.H.A. Training party GROUP served "D" halted at BUIRE and one to be unlimited W. SANDYS CMG. 29th Bde R.H.A. & remained Group — 4th motor lorries of Bde. Gen. GEDDES CRA. 5th Divn —	
9th	Both Btys. moved to permanent billets D's in BERNANCOURT and chestnuts SUZANNE. Btys. commenced rigging covers frames his whole this is little inducement the tunnelling into has been made to estimate an 8 shell hole. from front Btys. were front in chiefly with him to explain German trucks on section 5.A.A. Divn. Austr. Gen. was sent to CONTAY from 2nd J/C.D. Austr. Gen. in order to supply the 51 Al. Rgt. Bde. — The lettr. Rgt. are noun known at MARTINSART to 2nd J/C.D. HQ lieutenant fort line — tunnel form HAMEL to AUTHUILLE	

Army Form C. 2118.

WAR DIARY
H Qs, 1st Ind. of R.H.A. Bde.
INTELLIGENCE SUMMARY.

(Erase heading not required.)

24
Last Appendix (15 c)

Hour, Date, Place.	Summary of Events and Information.	Remarks and references to Appendices.
Aug. 1915 23rd LA HAIE	Orders rec'd from 2nd Cav. Corps to remainder of 1st & 2nd R.H.A. Bde. to hold itself in readiness to move from 5th Division. Col. Rouse accompanied Gen. Robinson up to III rd Army Hq.s. where it was arranged that "U" Bty, with Adjut: between 1st Div. Ansb. Car. should join Col. Fitzmaurice's group in neighbourhood of SUZANNE. "U" Bty. less one section, marched at 8 A.M. to bivouac in	
24th	woods 1/2 mile N.W. of CHIPILLY. One section going into action N. of Suzanne	
	orders rec'd from 2nd Cav. Corps notifying	
26th	Major W.A. Eden D.S.O. Captain the 27th Curry RHA to command a Bde. R.H.A. heading momentum. Captain W.A. Nicholls from "V" Battery R.H.A. succeeded him in commanding "Q" Battery R.H.A. Captain A.W. van STRAUBENZEE, Adjutant, 1st Bde R.H.A. to join "V" Battery Lieut. F.C.B. Dale from "V" Battery R.H.A. succeeded Capt. A.W. van STRAUBENZEE as adjutant. "U" Battery moved into action N. of Suzanne and came under orders of Right Group V th Division	

G.Ode Lt. Col. 1st/2nd R.H.A. Brigade
1st Indian R.H.A. Brigade

Serial No. 64.

Confidential

121/286

War Diary

of

Head Quarters, 1st Indian R.A. Brigade.

FROM 1st September 1915. TO 30th September 1915.

Army Form C. 2118.

25

last appendix (15C.)

WAR DIARY
or
INTELLIGENCE SUMMARY.
(Erase heading not required.)

Hour, Date, Place.	Summary of Events and Information.	Remarks and references to Appendices.
LA HAIE SYRCAMP'S Sept 5-	S.A.A. section of 12th Indian Cavalry Divisional Ammunition Column previously attached to 2nd Indian Cavalry Divisional Ammunition Column returned to SIALKOTE Brigade.	
Sept 7th	Lieut: E.C.B.DALE arrived at headquarters from 'U' Battery R.H.A.	
Sept 9th	New S.A.A. Sections of 12th Indian Cavalry Divisional Ammunition Column moved to BETHENCOURT (ref: AMIENS 1/80000 map) in accordance with orders of change of billeting area. ST OUEN (mt nt at nt an dm), ST HILAIRE, LANCHES, being allotted to 'A','U',Q Batteries R.H.A in the order named, but not occupied	
Sept 12th	Lieut C.F.CAMPBELL left Brigade Headquarters to join 'U' Battery R.H.A	
Sept 13th – 14th	During the night relieving portions of Batteries marched to their wagon lines	90.-

Army Form C. 2118.

26

WAR DIARY
or
INTELLIGENCE SUMMARY.
(Erase heading not required.)

Appendix (15.C)

Hour, Date, Place.	Summary of Events and Information.	Remarks and references to Appendices.
LA HAIE SUR CAMPS		
Sept 14-15	Batteries & sections of Divisional Ammunition Column attached to them moved to Billets at FRECHENCOURT (ref. AMIENS 1/80000 map)	
Sept 15	Batteries & sections of Column attached reached Billets 'A' Battery at ST OUEN, 'Q' Battery at LANCHES, 'U' Battery at ST HILAIRE	
Sept 17	Genl BARROW Commanding 1st Indian Cavalry Division Visited A Battery and Brig. Ammunition Column Lieut J.K. BOOTHBY joined 'U' Battery R.H.A. from 11 Genl BARROW visited Q & U Batteries	Memorandum received from III Army conveying appreciation given for 2 R.H.A. Batteries while in action under III Army.
Sept 18.		
Sept 20	Divisional Staff and C.R.A. and Battery Commanders took part in Training Scheme over ground between ST OUEN and GORENFLOS	
Sept 21	Divisional Field day was to have taken place but the scheme was cancelled and Indian Cavalry Corps was inspected by LORD KITCHENER.	

Army Form C. 2118.

WAR DIARY
or
INTELLIGENCE SUMMARY.
(Erase heading not required.)

2-7

Last appendices (15.C.)

Hour, Date, Place.	Summary of Events and Information.	Remarks and references to Appendices.
Sept 22nd	Divisional scheme postponed from the 21st was to have taken place but was cancelled owing to the Divin not moving. R.H.A Brigade starting Point was to have been at X roads 200 yards S. of ES of LANCHES owing to orders not being received. Batteries and not the warned in time and were ordered to move independently to HEUZECOURT when they were to billet. Remaining troops that were to come under orders of Colonel Home also moved independently. Whole Brigade had moved independently into Billets by 5.15 p.m.	
HEUZECOURT Sept 24th	Reconnaissance of crossings of river AUTHIE at HEM, OCCOCHES, OUTREBOIS carried out by officers of A, Q and U Batteries respectively. In afternoon an officer from "Q" & "U" Batteries were sent to report on roads & tracks Between BARLY & AVESNES-LE-COMTE.	
Sept 25-	Orders received from 1st Indian Cavalry Division for spare Kits to be 'dumped'. 'B' Echelon wagons being sent to draw two days supplies from DOULLENS & 'A' Echelon wagons	

Army Form C. 2118.

28 (vide appendices 15. C.)

WAR DIARY
or
INTELLIGENCE SUMMARY.
(*Erase heading not required.*)

Instructions regarding War Diaries and Intelligence Summaries are contained in F. S. Regs., Part II, and the Staff Manual respectively. Title pages will be prepared in manuscript.

Hour, Date, Place.	Summary of Events and Information.	Remarks and references to Appendices.
HEUZECOURT Sept 25th	showing two days emergency rations

G.W. Wright
1st Indian R.H.A. Brigade | |

Serial No. 49.

Confidential
121/7601

War Diary

of

Head Quarters

1st Indian R.H.A. Brigade.

FROM 1st October 1915. **TO** 31st October 1915.

Army Form C. 2118.

29

LAST APPENDIX 15 C

WAR DIARY
or
INTELLIGENCE SUMMARY.
(Erase heading not required.)

Place	Date	Hour	Summary of Events and Information	Remarks and references to Appendices
HEUZECOURT	1:10:15		Divisional Exercise took place, all troops out; the Divisional Ammunition Column moved their billets from Mt REMANT to ST ACHEUL.	
"	5:10:15		Divisional Exercise. All troops out except the Divisional Ammunition Column which only came out in skeleton.	
"	8:10:15		Divisional Exercise in continuation of the scheme of Oct: 5th.	
"	10:10:15		Division issued orders to effect that Brigades were at 10 hours notice.	
"	13:10:15		R.H.A. Brigade moved billets to VAUCHELLES CHAU. "A" Battery to ST HILAIRE, "Q" Battery to LE MEILLARD, "U" Battery to AUTHEUX. Div. Ammn Coln to VAUCHELLES & MOUFLERS	
VAUCHELLES	15:10:15		Divisional Exercise. All troops out except Brig. Ammn Coln.	
"	18:10:15		Divisional Reserve	
SOUES	22:10:15		Division moved to new area S. of R. SOMME. R.H.A. Headquarters at SOUES, Batteries with their Cavalry Brigades; as follows:—	

Army Form C. 2118.

WAR DIARY
or
INTELLIGENCE SUMMARY.
(Erase heading not required.)

Last appendices — 15C.

Instructions regarding War Diaries and Intelligence Summaries are contained in F. S. Regs., Part II. and the Staff Manual respectively. Title pages will be prepared in manuscript.

Place	Date	Hour	Summary of Events and Information	Remarks and references to Appendices
SOUES	22.10.15		A Battery R.H.A at ETREJUST. Q Battery at FOUDRINOY. Captain H. WALKER + Captain A. G. ROLLESTON report at War office to take over new Batteries and left for England on 23rd.	
	27.10.15		All batteries out for preliminary review by Colonel Home before being inspected by His Majesty owing to the accident to His Majesty the review did not take place.	

Walter Jones of 11th Indian R.H.A. Brigade

1577 Wt.W10791/1773 500,000 1/15 D. D. & L. A.D.S.S./Forms/C. 2118.

Serial No. 49.

121/1180

Confidential

War Diary

of

1st Indian R.H.A. Brigade.

FROM 1st November 1915 TO 30th November 1915

Army Form C. 2118.

WAR DIARY
or
INTELLIGENCE SUMMARY.
(Erase heading not required.)

Place	Date	Hour	Summary of Events and Information	Remarks and references to Appendices
SOUES	Nov. 4		Captain L.C. WHITE left "A" Battery R.H.A. to take over command of a battery of the 27th Division.	
"	Nov. 8		Division paraded for distribution of French Distinctions by Corps Commander. Major R.H. LASCELLES Received Legion of Honour 5th Class + Corporal NOKES Croix de Guerre both the above were from "U" Battery R.H.A.	
"	Nov. 9		Gen: RIMINGTON inspected Divisional Ammunition Park.	
"	Nov. 11		Gen: Sir E. ALLENBY inspected the Corps near Le QUESNOY.	
CROQUOISON	Nov. 18		Moved into new billets at CROQUOISON. "A" Battery remained at AVESNES. "Q" moved to EPAUMAISNIL; "U" moved to BETTENCOURT. Column remained. Div. Park moved to AIRAINES.	
"	" 20		"U" Battery moved to MEIGNY	
"	" 21		Major SCOTT A.S.C. left Div. Park to take command of MEERUT Supply Column	
"	" 22		Captain HOWARD arrived to take over command of 4th Ind. Cav. Brig. Ammn. Park.	

Army Form C. 2118.

WAR DIARY
or
INTELLIGENCE SUMMARY.
(Erase heading not required.)

Last offensive — 15.C.

Place	Date	Hour	Summary of Events and Information	Remarks and references to Appendices
CROIQUOISON	Nov 23		Genl. M. RIMINGTON inspected the Remounts of the R.H.A. Brigade that had arrived with the Brigade since Sept. 1st 1915.	

9 late Staff
1st Indian R.H.A. Brigade

SERIAL NO. 49.

Confidential
War Diary
of

1st Indian F.A. Brigade.

FROM 1st December 1915 TO 31st December 1915.

WAR DIARY
1st INDIAN * R.H.A Brigade
INTELLIGENCE SUMMARY

Army Form C. 2118.

LAST APPENDIX - 15 C.

Place	Date	Hour	Summary of Events and Information	Remarks and references to Appendices
CROQUOISON	4/12/15		Orders received for Lieuts DALE and SIMPSON to proceed to II and IV Division at CHOCQUES and MANDICOURT PAS respectively. Lieut HUGGINS and MARTIN to act as Captains pending promotion Auty A778 of 4/12/15	
" - "	5/12/15		Lieut DALE left for CHOCQUES. Departure reported.	
" - "	6/12/15		Information received (GA a94) that two Batteries R.H.A and two thirds Gun Section D.A.C moved shortly move for duty with 10th Corps. - One with 5th Division and one with 18th Division. 14" and U Batteries detailed respectively.	
" - "	7/12/15		"A" Battery ordered to join V Division on 8th to field night of 8/9 at CARDONNETTE and night of 9/10 at LANEUVILLE. 1/3 Gun Section of D.A.C to move with Battery. Received Amendments (Secret) to War Establishments of Armoured Divisions. Extracts forwarded to Batteries, D.A.C and Ammunition Park Orders that U Battery with 1/3 Gun Section D.A.C will move on 10th	
" - "	8/12/15		A Battery moved with to join V Division to Section D.A.C ordered to join up at CARDONNETTE Lieut STAVELEY R.H.A (A Battery) R.H.A ordered to join IV Division pending promotion to Captain into Lieut SIMPSON Q Battery who remains with Division. Lieut McKAY Reported to 17 Battery R.H.A	
" - "	9/12/15		Lieut STAVELEY departed for (ACHEUX) IV Division. Departure reported. 1/3 Section (Gun) D.A.C joined up with U Battery at METIGNE for move on 10th	
" - "	9-12-15		U Battery R.H.A with 1/3 Gun Section D.A.C moved from METIGNE. One Section of Battery joining 51st Division remainder joining 18th Division	
" - "	10.12.15		Sgt GH ROUSE RHA D.S.O with Major PAYNTER RHA Q Battery R.H.A attended conference at Div H.Q in connection with a scheme for trench warfare. Lt Col ROUSE'S 2nd Charger destroyed, having been run into by Motor Car at EPAUMESNIL while exercising on 2-12-15. Veterinary Officer decided no hopes of recovery from fracture hoof. Numbers of Car (taken by R. Gale, groom.) Enquiries made but no trace of car.	

Army Form C. 2118.

WAR DIARY
1ST INDIAN OR R.H.A. BRIGADE.
INTELLIGENCE SUMMARY.
(Erase heading not required.)

34

LAST APPENDIX 15 C

Place	Date	Hour	Summary of Events and Information	Remarks and references to Appendices
CROQUOISON	11/12/15		Lt. Col. H. Rouse RHA DSO proceeds on leave to England	
	-"-		Lt. Howard. Q. Bay. R.H.A. deputes to attend Trench Warfare Class Commencing 20/12/15 (amended on 23/12/15)	
	15/12/15		Orders received for Head Quarters, 1st Indian R.H.A. Brigade and Divisional Ammunition Column to move on 16th to BEAUCHAMPS - Head Quarters to move via OISEMONT and GAMACHES. Ammunition Park to move to BOULLANCOURT	
	16/12		Head Quarters left billets at 9.30 a.m. and marched via ST MAULVIS, OISEMONT, GAMACHES. Roads very heavy between ST MAULVIS and OISEMONT. Watered and fed at LE TRANSLAY at 12 noon. Continued march at 12/40 pm reaching BEAUCAMPS at 2.20 pm. Arrival reported to 1st Ind. Car. Division Head Quarters. Authority received from 2nd Cav. Corps for appointment of Lieut. HOWARD Q/13th RHB as Adjutant	
BEAUCHAMPS	16/12/15		Orders received for Lt. Col. H. Rouse. R.H.A. D.S.O to join 37th Division to Command 124 R.J.A Brigade. He will be replaced by St. Col C.F.C.G. CHARLTON from 37th Division on 20/12/15	
	17/12/15		Lt. Col. H. Rouse. R.H.A. D.S.O left for 37th Division at 9 am. (proceeding by car to PAS (8 miles E of DOULLENS)	
	20/12/15		Orders received that Trench Warfare Class would not commence until 27th Dec 15.	
	21/12/15		St. Col C.E.G.G. CHARLTON arrives in relief of Col H. Rouse. Arrival reported.	
	22/12/15		All horses (except 3) feet for Glanders by Capt MAYNARD. A.V.C. (The 3 were tested on 26th inst.)	
	23/12/15		Allotment of grenades for training purposes received as follows:-	
			SIALKOT. MHOW. LUCKNOW FIELD SQDN	
			No 1 13 13 13 9 = 48 } to be drawn and distributed by	
			5 500 500 500 75 = 1575 } Ammunition Park at the beginning of each month. A.P. notifies HE/Lieut.	
			The name of Lt. WOOD Q/B of R.H.A. substitutes for that of Lieut Howard to attend Trench Warfare Class commencing on 27/12/15. Date amended to 29/12/15	

Army Form C. 2118.

WAR DIARY
1ST INDIAN or R.H.A. BRIGADE
INTELLIGENCE SUMMARY.

(Erase heading not required.)

Place	Date	Hour	Summary of Events and Information	Remarks and references to Appendices
BEAUCAMPS	25 12/15		Day passed very quietly. N.C.O. and men, having received a Supply of Christmas Puddings from Col ROUSE (before his departure) S/Col CHARLTON and from Supply Officer and other Seasonable Extras (including Champagne from the Manager of the factory in which they are billeted) had a fairly enjoyable day. The Divisional Ammunition Column gave a very successful Concert in the evening at which a large number of the inhabitants were invited. The O.C. Brigade visited the Concert during the evening.	1ST APPENDIX 15 c
"	28/12/15		The Head Quarter Staff paraded in Marching Order and seen by Commanding Officer. They were then taken for 1½ hours Route March, particular attention being paid to March discipline.	
"	29/12/15		All H.Q. Horses passed as free from Glanders. Capt SIMPSON R.H.A. (in the absence of MAJOR PAYNTER R.H.A. on leave) visited O.C. Brigade and arranged details for Bakery Parade for 30th inst, when they will be seen by the O.C. Brigade.	
"	30/12/15		Q Bakery R.H.A. seen by Lt Col CHARLTON. R.H.A. on parade	
"	31/12/15		S/Col CHARLTON. R.H.A. attended inspection of Mhow Brigade by Corps Commander	

J.E. Westropp [?] S/Lt R.A.
Adjutant
1st Division R.H.A. Brigade

SERIAL No. 49

Confidential

War Diary

of

Headquarters 1st Indian F.A. Brigade.

FROM 1st January 1915 TO 31st January 1915

Army Form C. 2118.

WAR DIARY
1ST INDIAN R.H.A. BRIGADE
INTELLIGENCE SUMMARY.

(Erase heading not required.)

LAST APPENDIX 15C

Place	Date	Hour	Summary of Events and Information	Remarks and references to Appendices
BEAUCHAMPS	1 Jan 1916		H.E. Ammunition held by Ammn: Park inspected by Ordnance Representative S/Col CHARLTON. R.H.A. inspected Divisional Ammunition Column — (less 2 gun' Sections in action with A and U Batteries). The Column was formed in Column of Route on Road INCHEVILLE — EU facing E the head of the column being just E of INCHEVILLE. The parade was well turned out in marching order — the majority of the Harness and Equipment being very clean and all in good repair. Divisional Marathon took place 15 day at 10-30 am. British Units teams of 10 and Indian Units teams of 40. Starting point WOINCOURT. Winning Post FRIERVILLE. Distance about 6 miles. Results:— The 1st R.H.A. Brigade did not compete. 1st 17 Lancers. 2nd 16 Dragoons. 3rd 1st K.D.G. INDIAN 1st 35, 2nd Lancers. 2nd 38th Horse. 3rd 6th Cavalry Marathon. Reading 8 am 29.9 8 pm 29.8	CM/55/16 CM/265/16 14/2/16
	2/1/16		Barometer Reading 8 am 30.1 8 pm 29.9 Orders received from O.C. A.S.C. to last Ins: Cav Divn that 1st Ammn Park would take over as at the disposal of O.C. R.H.A. Bde, and that cars would not be detailed for duty without notifying O.C. Brigade. Original memo to O.C. 1st Ammn Park Copy Attd. In a Supplement to the "London Gazette" published in the Times received 15 day dated War Office January 1st 1916 the following were mentioned in Dispatches by Sir J.D.P. French and dated Nov. 30th 1915 :— Lt Col H. ROUSE. R.H.A. D.S.O. Capt A.W. VAN STRAUBENZEE (late Adjutant) Major R.H. LASCELLES. O.C. U Battery R.H.A. Lieut E.C.B. DALE. U Bty R.H.A. Lieut R. STAVELEY A Bty R.H.A. H.E. Ammunition held by Q Battery R.H.A. inspected by Ordnance Representative. 3 Chargers arrived from Haase for O.C. Brigade.	

Army Form C. 2118.

WAR DIARY or INTELLIGENCE SUMMARY.

1st Indian R.H.A. Brigade 37

LAST APPENDIX 15 C.

(Erase heading not required.)

Place	Date	Hour	Summary of Events and Information	Remarks and references to Appendices
BEAUCHAMPS.	3rd/16		Barometer reading 8am 30.2 8pm 30.3	
			H.E. Ammunition fired by Dir. Amm. Column inspected by ORDNANCE Representative.	
			He recommended that all fuzes should be treated with lubric and all shells oiled occasionally.	
			This referred to all ammunition in the Brigade.	
	4th/16		Lt Col CHARLTON granted leave to proceed to ENGLAND via BOLOGNE and FOLKESTONE 3rd to 11th.	
			Barometer reading 8am 30.2 8pm 30.2 Lt Howard joined as Adjutant.	
	5th/16		Barometer reading 8am 30.3 8pm 30.1	
	6th/16		Barometer reading 8am 30.2 8pm 30.1	
			O.C. A.S.C. inspected G.S. Wagons, Limbers, Col. Wagons Handcart of 1st Armd Column.	
	7th/16		Barometer reading 8am 30.2 8pm 30.0	
	8th/16		" " 11 " 30.1 8pm 30.0	
	9th/16		" " 8am 29.8 8pm 30.3	
	10th/16		" " 8am 30.3 8pm 30.2	
	11th/16		" " 8am 30.1 8pm 30.2	
	12th/16		" " 8am 30.2 8pm 30.1	
			Genl M. Rimington, Commanding Indian Cav: Corps inspects Q Battery R.H.A. in Marching Order near ACHEUX	
	13th/16		Barometer Reading 8am 28.8 8pm	

Army Form C. 2118.

1st INDIAN ex R.H.A. Bde 38
WAR DIARY or INTELLIGENCE SUMMARY.
(Erase heading not required.)

Last Appendix 15c

Instructions regarding War Diaries and Intelligence Summaries are contained in F.S. Regs., Part II and the Staff Manual respectively. Title pages will be prepared in manuscript.

Place	Date	Hour	Summary of Events and Information	Remarks and references to Appendices
BEAUCHAMPS	16/1/16		Canadian Cavalry Brigade joins Bde.	
	17/1/15		Col CHARLTON visits A and U Batteries in action	

J E Westrope Lt R.H.A
for ADJUTANT, R.H.A.
1st INDIAN R.H.A. BRIGADE.

SERIAL No. 49

Confidential

War Diary

of

1st Indian R.H.A. Brigade

FROM 1st February 1916 TO 29th February 1916

WAR DIARY of 1st INDIAN R.H.A. Bde
INTELLIGENCE SUMMARY.

Army Form C. 2118.

Place	Date	Hour	Summary of Events and Information	Remarks and references to Appendices
BEAUCHAMPS.	4 Feby /16		Lieut Hopkins (S.R) and Lieut Ivens (S.R) arrive. Attached to 'Q' Battery R.H.A. U Battery R.H.A. on coming out of action near ALBERT, billeted the night of 4th–5th at CONDIE FOLIE with proportion of D.A.C and Ammn Park en route to permanent billets. U Battery at OCHANCOURT. D.A.C at BEAUCHAMPS. Ammn Park at BOUILLANCOURT.	
	10/16		Reports received from Brigr. Genl (R.A) 8th GEDDES. Commanding R.A 10th Corps recording his appreciation of the way A and U Batteries carried out their duties during the time they were under his command. Lt Col T.L.N MORLAND Commanding 10th Corps expresses his appreciation in the same report.	
	13/16		A Battery on coming out of action the night of 13/14 at CONDIE – FOLIE with Section of D.F.C.	
	14/16		A Battery moved to permanent billets at NABAS. Section of D.A.C. joined its Head Qrs at BEAUCHAMPS.	
OFFEUX	16/16		Brigade Head Qrs moved from BEAUCHAMPS to OFFEUX Brig Genl LEADER, Commdg 1st I.C. Div. inspected horses of A and U Battery	
	17/16		2nd Ind. R.H.A Bde. left Corps Area for MERVILLE.	
	23rd		Lt. Hopkins and Lt. IVENS left Q Battery for 2nd Ind. Cav Div. Lt J. C. ELLIS. (S.R) Lt. C.H. THORNHILL. (S.R) and Lt. F. WILDER joined from ENGLAND and attached to Batteries as follows: – ELLIS to A. Bty. THORNHILL and WILDER to Q Bty.	
	29 / 2 / 1916			J Westrope Lt RHA for Adjt 1st Indian RHA Brigade

SERIAL NO. 4 9.

Confidential

War Diary

of

1st Indian R.H.A. Brigade Headquarters

FROM 1st March 1916 **TO** 31st March 1916.

Army Form C. 2118.

WAR DIARY

1st Indian or R.H.A. BRIGADE

INTELLIGENCE SUMMARY

(Erase heading not required.)

Read Appendix 15 C

Place	Date	Hour	Summary of Events and Information	Remarks and references to Appendices
OFFEUX	27/3/16		Notification that B.Q.M. Sgt C.S. YOUNGS. Q Battery R.H.A. and B.Q.M. Sgt Copley U Battery, R.H.A. were appointed Field with effect from 27-2-1916.	
	3		Confidential notification that Cavalry Corps and INDIAN CAV. CORPS will be abolished as both Divisions allotted as Reserves as follows:— 1st Cavalry Division — to 1st Army. 2nd " — to 2nd " 1st Indian Cav. " — to 3rd " 2nd " — to 4th " The 3rd Cavalry Division together with the CANADIAN CAV. BDE. will form a Reserve under G.H.Q.	
	23		Q Battery R.H.A. proceeded to HAUTECLOQUE to take over 18 pr guns of 122 Bty R.F.A. Relieves night of 23/24 at WILLENCOURT. On arrival at HAUTECLOQUE to come under orders of C.R.A. 5th Division.	
	25		1st I.C. Div. moved into new area. 1st Ind R.H.A. Bde H.Qrs moving on 26th. Relieves night of 26/27 at NEUF-MOULIN with Div Amm. Column.	
QUOEUX	27		Moved into permanent billets at QUOEUX.	
	31/3/1916			

J Westropp Lt R.J.A.
for Adj. R.H.A.
1st Ind R.H.A. Bde. H.Q Qrs

SERIAL NO. 49.

Confidential

War Diary

of

1st Indian R.H.A. Brigade Headquarters

FROM 1st April 1916 **TO** 30th April 1916.

Army Form C. 2118.

WAR DIARY

1st INDIAN R.H.A. Bde 41

INTELLIGENCE SUMMARY.

LAST APPENDIX 15-C

(Erase heading not required.)

Instructions regarding War Diaries and Intelligence Summaries are contained in F. S. Regs., Part II. and the Staff Manual respectively. Title pages will be prepared in manuscript.

Place	Date	Hour	Summary of Events and Information	Remarks and references to Appendices
QUOEUX	1-4-1916		Col CHARLTON visits Corps line with Division Commander	
	2-4-	"	Death of 2" F. WILDER (attached R/Bty RHA) reported in "TIMES" Killed in action	
		"	(R/HA Pole Head Qrs with One Section of D.A.C. marched to St RIQUIER Training Area Bivouacs at MILLENCOURT	
	15/4/16		'A' Battery and one Section of D.A.C. marched to area & billets at ARGENVILLERS. 'U' Battery already there. The whole to take part in R.H.A Pole training. 15th to 22nd	
	16/4/16		The training programme included :- Map reading tests, Movements of Vehicles across Country. Battery leading by Subalterns and Brigade Tactical Exercises	
	22nd		Mhow Bde and 11/1 Head Qrs marched into training area.	
	30th		Section 'S' R.A.C at St GEORGES moved into MILLENCOURT for training, the Section then at MILLENCOURT returning to St GEORGES.	
			Notification that 12 guns & 12 limbers (18 pr) due at AUXI on 1-5-1916 with instructions to clear at once and return to 13 pr.	
			Memo from 1st I.C.D. asking if Major MELLOR A/RHA recommended to Command R.F.A Pole. Reply "Yes"	
			Col CHARLTON visits Head Qrs Army St POL.	

FIELD
30/4/1916

J Westropp ... ?
for ADJUTANT, R.H.A.
1st INDIAN R.H.A. BDE ...

1577 Wt.W10791/1773 500,000 1/15 D. D. & L. A.D.S.S./Forms/C. 2118.

SERIAL NO. 49.

Confidential
War Diary
of

1st Indian Royal Horse Artillery Brigade

FROM 1st May 1916 TO 31st May 1916.

Army Form C. 2118.

WAR DIARY
1ST INDIAN 1st R.H.A. Bde 42
INTELLIGENCE SUMMARY
Last Appendix 15 C

(Erase heading not required.)

Place	Date	Hour	Summary of Events and Information	Remarks and references to Appendices
MILLENCOURT	5/7/16		Artillery	
	5/7/16		Following 18 pdr arrived at AUXI-LE-CHATEAU	
			A Batty R.H.A 6 Guns & 12 Wagons	
	6/7/16		U " " 6 Guns & 12 Wagons	
			D.A.C. 18 Wagons	
	8/7/16	5.	1st Ammn Col returned to permanent billets on completion of training	
			H. Qrs and Batteries returned to permanent billets	
			Major DUDLEY arrived from 124th Bde R.F.A relieved Major A MELLOR R.H.A. of Chestnut Troop. Major MELLOR left to command 90th Bde R.F.A. as Lieut St Col on 5th inst.	
QUDEUX	10th		The Brigade moved into new billets as follows. Bde Head Qrs LIENCOURT. A By to BROUILLY	
			U By to Rebreurette D.A. Col to ETREE WAMIN.	
	18th		Head Qrs moved to VILLERSCHATEL. A.U and D.A.C. to MINGOVAL.	
	19th		2 Sections of 'U' By went into action taking over position of D/111 Bde.	
	20th		2 Sections of 'A' By went into action	
	21st		Head Qrs moved to MAROEUIL.	
	26th		2 Sections of 'U' By relieved by D/111 By	
	27th		U By Commenced preparing new position	
	28th		2 Guns of 'A' into action, completing the Battery.	
	29th		2 Guns of 'U' into newly prepared position	
	30th		2 " " " " " "	
	31/7		Bde Head Qrs moved into 111 Bde Head Qrs about 3½ Miles N.W of ARRAS.	

31/7
1/9/16
J.G. Wearly, RHA
Lt Col, for Brig Genl

SERIAL NO. 49.

Confidential
Diary
of

Hd. Qrs., 1st Indian F. H. A. Brigade.

FROM 1st June 1916 TO 30th June 1916.

Army Form C. 2118.

WAR DIARY
1/ INDIAN RHA or Brigade
INTELLIGENCE SUMMARY

43

(Erase heading not required.)

Place	Date	Hour	Summary of Events and Information	Remarks and references to Appendices
FIELD	June 3rd		A4U + @ Bty and D.A.C wagon lines moved to Acq.	
			Since being in action the Head Qrs have commenced new dugouts. Batteries improving their gun pits and O.Ps and preparing alternatives.	
	14		Lt. G.F.R. LENANTON appointed to R.H.A. + posted to @ Bty R.H.A.	
	15		Smoke helmets received with Sponge eyepieces (10)	
	14		Clock hour advance 1 hour at 11 pm.	
	21		Asst. Surgeon Needs from Batteries + D.A.C. on transfer to India.	
	28th		Lt. R.A. QUINN, from SIALKOT C.F.A arrived at Bge Hd Qrs as M.O.	
	29th		He rode came out of action without casualties. Marching to Acq. remaining here until 5/30 pm.	
	29th		Bde marched to Riellets at:- Head Qrs + Q Bty- VILLERS SIRE SIMON. A at BLAVINCOURT. U at REBREUVE. D.A.C at ETREE WAMIN.	
	30th		Heavy baggage and Stores not required were taken by lorries to Divisional Dump at LE CAUROY. Bge marched independently to DOULLENS. Men were billeted in close gardens in town and lorries in Citadel Moat. Bge Head Qrs at DOULLENS.	

1/4/16

F Weatlife LRfr
Adjutant, R.H.A.
1st Indian R.H. Brigade

SERIAL NO. 49.

Confidential
War Diary
of

Headquarters 1st Indian F.H.A. Brigade.

FROM 1st July 1916 TO 31st July 1916.

H.Q. R.H.A. BDE.

Army Form C. 2118

WAR DIARY
1st INDIAN R.H.A. or BRIGADE
INTELLIGENCE SUMMARY.
(Erase heading not required.)

44

Place	Date	Hour	Summary of Events and Information	Remarks and references to Appendices
DOULLENS	2/16		The Division received orders to be prepared to move at 2½ hours notice	
	6th		Orders received by R.H.A. Bde. Head Qrs at 3/45 p.m. to march to new area at 5-30 p.m. Brigade moved to new Billets as follows:- Head Qrs CHATEAU DRUCAS (WAVANS) A.Q. and U Batteries and D.A. Col. at WAVANS and BEAUVOIR RIVIERE /EW	
BOUVOIR RIVIERE WAVANS	10th		Annual Horse Show and sports held by 'U' Battery in their lines /EW Rev Winsfield Digby (A.C.) arrives at Bde Head Qrs /EW	
	11th		Division under 8 hours notice /EW	
	12th		Lieut P.L. GRAHAM arrived from the Base and posted to Q' Bty RHA /EW	
	16th		Information received that one Battery of the Brigade would be attached to 5th Bde /EW 'U' Battery warned with Section of D.A.C. to hold themselves in readiness	
	17th		U Battery and one gun section of D.A.C. moved to TALMAS to come under orders of 5th Division A.J. Lieut BENNEE. R.A.M.C. attached to Brit Army Col as M.O. to Amm Col /EW	
	19/14		R.H.A. Bde (less 'U' Battery and Section of D.A.C.) moved to new area as follows to come under orders of XVII Corps. 60th (London) Division. Billets the night at ECUIVRES /EW	
	20th		Battery Wagon lines moved to FREVIN CAPEL Head Quarters moved to TROIS MAISON, MARCEUIL /EW	

Army Form C. 2118

WAR DIARY
or
INTELLIGENCE SUMMARY.
(Erase heading not required.) 4 5

Instructions regarding War Diaries and Intelligence Summaries are contained in F.S. Regs., Part II. and the Staff Manual respectively. Title pages will be prepared in manuscript.

Place	Date	Hour	Summary of Events and Information	Remarks and references to Appendices
	20/6		2 Sections of 'A' Battery went into action by night.	
	21/6		2 Sections of 'Q' Batty went into action by night. JEW	
	25/6		Remaining Sections (A & Q Btries) into action by night. JEW	
			Received news (unofficial) that 'U' Battery has been having a bad time and that Lieut Clarke Williams, O/C Section of, & a Col had been sent up to Battery, being relieved temporarily by an Officer of the 5th Brl Amm Col. JEW	
	26/6		Lt W.K. Holmes sent up from 1st Amm Col to 'U' Battery.	
			Lt Clarke-Williams rejoins Hd Qrs of 1st Amm Col. JEW	
	30/6		1st Ind Cav Div reported that Lt BRAITHWAITE was killed on 22nd. Lieut BOOTHBY killed on 23rd. Lt CAMPBELL and two other ranks wounded on 25th. All the above were in action with 'U' Bty R.H.A. JEW	
TROIS MAISON (MAROEUIL)	31st		Allotment of Ammunition for Period ending 9 August. A 100 A×900 Lo	

J.E. Westropse Lt R.H.A
for Lieut Col R.H.A.
Commanding R.H.A Bde
1st Ind Cav Division

Commanding R.H.A Bde
1st Ind Cav Division

SERIAL NO. 49

Confidential
War Diary
of

Headquarters 1st Indian R.H.A. Brigade.

FROM 1st August 1916 TO 31st August 1916.

Army Form C. 2118.

R.H.A. **WAR DIARY**
Brigadier Hd Qrs, 1st Indian Cavy Division
INTELLIGENCE SUMMARY.
(Erase heading not required.)

40

Place	Date	Hour	Summary of Events and Information	Remarks and references to Appendices
MARŒUIL	August 1/15 1st		Batteries still in action in same positions. Very little firing beyond "Registering". Employed chiefly in preparing new positions — One Gunner "U" Bty wounded in action	JEW
	2nd		Two bombs were dropped by HUN planes near MARŒUIL Railway Station at 5/0 am. No damage done. JEW	
	3rd		Wire received asking if Major LASCELLES recommended to command a Brigade R.F.A. If so he would be required to join 1st Division at once — Reply wired Yes. Br. CHAPMAN "U" Batty wounded in action. Orders received that owing to 21st Division likely to be short of some guns until arrival of some from England — the III Army Commdr has decided to reinforce 21st Division with Hd Qrs Batteries. (in case of emergency) B Co to report to 16 (A Co 6th Corps at 9.30 am on Hd Qrs to reconnoitre positions (afterwards amended to 5th mid.)	
	3rd		ACQ shelled about 10.30 pm about 25 rounds falling in and about village. Horses of 'Q' Battery were removed to about 100ᵡ out of village necessary precautions were taken by 'A' Bty wagon lines and D.A.C in case range was increased — No damage done to either wagon lines. JEW	
	4th		Owing to number of new positions to be prepared by Batteries 6 men were sent up from D.A.C to assist each Battery. Six Gunners and Six Drivers sent up to "U" Bty (including 3 telephonists) from D.A.C pending arrival of reinforcements. JEW	

R.H.A. Brigade Head Qrs.
WAR DIARY
INTELLIGENCE SUMMARY.

1st Ind Cavy Division

Army Form C. 2118.

47

(Erase heading not required.)

Place	Date Hour	Summary of Events and Information	Remarks and references to Appendices
MARŒUIL	August 1916 5th 8/45 am	Lt Col Commanding, accompanied by MAJOR PAYNTER ('Q' Bty.) and MAJOR DUDLEY ('A' Bty) left by motor car to report to Head Qrs, 5th Corps to reconnoitre positions allotted to Batteries	
	12.30 pm	One gun of Y Battery destroyed and one Gun & one lorry badly damaged by enemy fire. One of our observation Balloons was hit by enemy shell fire. The two observers took to their parachutes and were seen descending softly. The balloon drifted gradually and descended slowly. FEW	
	6th	A raid of the German trenches was carried out about 10 pm. Q Battery being called upon at a late hour to take the place of a Battery R.F.A. (Left Group) which has been having a warm time during the morning (2 men killed and one gun put out of action) Two prisoners were brought over by the raiders. FEW	
	7th	A raid on the German trenches commenced at 9.30 pm A. Battery assisted - firing about 150 A. and 50 A.X. Information received that in addition to the casualties recorded on No 45 'U' Battery had the following:- 29/76 Lt SJ. KEMM and Lt. W.K. HOLMES two wounded. On 23/76 3 R & O 5 men wounded. 24/76 1 Gr. Killed and 1 Gr. wounded. 25/76 1 Gr. Killed 2 Sergts and 5 Grs Wounded. On 26/76 2 wounded. On 28/76 One wounded. 26/76 2 Ammuntn Wagons destroyed 29th 1 Horse Killed & FEW	

Army Form C. 2118.

WAR DIARY
R.H.A. Brigade Head Qtrs (1st Indian Cav. Div.)
INTELLIGENCE SUMMARY.

(Erase heading not required.)

48

Instructions regarding War Diaries and Intelligence Summaries are contained in F. S. Regs., Part II. and the Staff Manual respectively. Title pages will be prepared in manuscript.

Place	Date	Hour	Summary of Events and Information	Remarks and references to Appendices
MARŒUIL	9/8/16	3.46 pm	Bombardment of the German lip of CHASSERY Crater by 180th Infantry Bde in which the Artillery of the Left Group (including Q By R.H.A) 4 — 2" T.M"cars & Stokes Guns took part. — H.M. King GEORGE V visited and Artillery Observation post at MONT ST ELOY during the afternoon.	JEW
	10th		Report from "U" By RHA that Major LASCELLES left for 1st Division on promotion to Lt Col.	JEW
	12th		Lieut E.J.S.COWLING posted from 'A' By RHA to 'U' Batty.	JEW
	13th		Major E.E. RICH arrived Raichad en route to 'U' Bty in relief of Major LASCELLES.	JEW
	18th		Lieut R.C.M. CROFTON R.F.A joined and posted to 'A' By RHA. Extract from List No 95 "Appointments etc by G.O.C-in-C dt 12 August 1916 To be Lt. 51711 Serj A.J. MINSON from Q By RHA 1/8/16	JEW

1577 Wt. W10791/1773 500,000 1/15 D. D. & L. A.D.S.S./Forms/C. 2118.

Army Form C. 2118.

WAR DIARY
of Hd's Qrs. R.H.A. 1st Mounted Cav. Div.
INTELLIGENCE SUMMARY.

(Erase heading not required.)

Instructions regarding War Diaries and Intelligence Summaries are contained in F. S. Regs., Part II. and the Staff Manual respectively. Title pages will be prepared in manuscript.

Place	Date	Hour	Summary of Events and Information	Remarks and references to Appendices
AUGUST 1916	18th		Sergt Woodham left D.A. Col (on promotion to Lieut.) for 11 Division. Date of Commission ? Authy III Army A.C. 5583/86 dt. 18/8/16. JEW	49
			During the whole month the Batteries have been employed chiefly in constructing new Gun Pits, O. Po's and laying and burying wire. JEW	
			L.E.W. Edestrope, Lt RHA Bde for Adjutant	
MARŒUIL	31/8/1916			

SERIAL NO. 49.

Confidential
War Diary
of

H. Qrs., 1st Indian Royal Horse Artillery Brigade.

FROM 1st September 1916 TO 30th September 1916

Army Form C. 2118.

WAR DIARY

~~INTELLIGENCE SUMMARY.~~

(Erase heading not required.)

Instructions regarding War Diaries and Intelligence Summaries are contained in F. S. Regs., Part II, and the Staff Manual respectively. Title pages will be prepared in manuscript.

CONFIDENTIAL

WAR DIARY

OF

R.H.A. Bde H.d Q.rs

from 1st Sept 1916 to 30 Sept 1916

Volume 1

Army Form C. 2118.

WAR DIARY

R.H.A. Brigade Head Quarters 1st Indian Cav Division

INTELLIGENCE SUMMARY.

(Erase heading not required.)

Instructions regarding War Diaries and Intelligence Summaries are contained in F. S. Regs., Part II, and the Staff Manual respectively. Title pages will be prepared in manuscript.

50

Hour, Date, Place.	Summary of Events and Information.	Remarks and references to Appendices.
September 1916. Marœuil 1st to 5th 6th 8.30 pm — 8/30 pm 7th 8/15 am 8th REBREUVE	Batteries still in action. Employed chiefly in constructing new Gun pits &c. JEW S.A.A. Section of D. A Column and part of Sub Ammn Column moved to Coulaville JEW One Section of 'A' and one section of 'Q' Battery out of action, marching to wagon lines. JEW ~~JEW Pts S. Quartier (deleted)~~ Remaining sections out of action, marching to wagon lines. JEW The Brigade marched to REBREUVE arriving 1 pm. Soon after leaving starting point the Brigade was seen by the Corps Commander (14th Corps) the C.R.A. both Divisions (B-G. Sinclair-Baikie) who at one time commanded the Chestnut troop. JEW	

Army Form C. 2118.

WAR DIARY
R.H.A. Bde Head Qrs, 1st I.S. Div

INTELLIGENCE SUMMARY.
(Erase heading not required.)   No 51

Hour, Date, Place.	Summary of Events and Information.	Remarks and references to Appendices.
Continued September 10th 1916		
REBREUVE 8/30 9th 9h	Brigade marched to BEALCOURT. Head Qrs at Château BEAUVOIR – arriving at 11 am the S.A.A. Section of 10. A.A. Column rejoined the Column. The Div Ammn Park is also billetted in BEALCOURT. JEW	
BEALCOURT		
DOULLENS 9 am 11th	Brigade marched to DOULLENS Divisional Head Qrs located at Hotel de Ville Brigade horses are in moat of Citadel. JEW	
FRECHENCOURT 13th	Brigade marched to new area and are bivouced just South of FRECHENCOURT or FRECHENCOURT – CARRIEU road Divisional Head Qrs. Brigades Head Qrs are located at ALLONVILLE JEW	
ALLONVILLE 14th	Lt. S.W. LEWIS reported to D.A. Col from 12th Division for attachment to R.H.A. Bde & is posted to D.A. Col JEW	

Army Form C. 2118.

WAR DIARY

R.H.A. Pde H&st Ar, 1st DC Divn

INTELLIGENCE SUMMARY.

No 52

(Erase heading not required.)

Hour, Date, Place.	Summary of Events and Information.	Remarks and references to Appendices.
September 1916 continued		
VILLE SUR ANCRE 15th	The Division now here in bivouacs (few tents) Divisional Head Qrs situated at MORLANCOURT the Heavy Section of D.A. Column left at FRECHENCOURT with A. & I. Coy which has been coupled with 18th. Ammunition and Spare gun parts en route. "U" Battery and Section of D.A Column rejoins the Brigade at CORBIE having been at rest a few days after a hot time at MONTAUBAN few.	
16th	Officers from Batteries and Coy B&co sent out to reconnoitre cavalry tracks forward to FRICOURT and MAMETZ. Division under 1 hour notice to move. Hot	
18th	Information received that Capt. HW HUGGINS D.S.O. has been granted Military Cross for good work during the time the Battery ("U") has been in the big Offensive — few.	

Army Form C. 2118.

WAR DIARY
RA Bde Hd Qrs 1st Ind Division
INTELLIGENCE SUMMARY.
(Erase heading not required.)

53

Instructions regarding War Diaries and Intelligence Summaries are contained in F. S. Regs., Part II, and the Staff Manual respectively. Title pages will be prepared in manuscript.

Continued

Hour, Date, Place.	Summary of Events and Information.	Remarks and references to Appendices.
September 1916 VILLE SUR ANCRE 14th	Division under 3 hours notice until further orders.	
25th	The Division (less Lucknow) moves to a preparatory position. Mhow Brigade with the Cheshire troops and Section of D.A. Column (less Heavy Section) to a position about midway between MONTAUBAN and LONGUEVAL. SIALKOT Cav Brigade and Q and U Batteries and Divisional Amm" Column just South of MAMETZ Divisional Advanced Report Centre at MONTAUBAN.	
MONTAUBAN and FRICOURT	C.R.H.A - Adjutant. Orderly Officer with telephone Cart and Signallers being in same place The Rear Report Centre of the Division and RHA Bde being at FRICOURT.	

Army Form C. 2118.

WAR DIARY

RHA Bde H/or(?) 1st S.? (?) 1 Division

INTELLIGENCE SUMMARY.

(Erase heading not required.)

54

Instructions regarding War Diaries and Intelligence Summaries are contained in F. S. Regs., Part II, and the Staff Manual respectively. Title pages will be prepared in manuscript.

Continued

Hour, Date, Place.	Summary of Events and Information.	Remarks and references to Appendices.
September 1916		
VILLE SUR ANCRE 26th Sept	About 6 pm orders were received that the Division would return to VILLE SUR ANCRE by the Cavalry track. A Battery and Section of D.A. Col to march under orders of MHOW Bde. JEW Orders received that Division would march to new area BUSSY les DOURS about 2 pm. Billeting parties were sent forward. As the Division (by Brigades) was moving off orders were received cancelling the move. LUCKNOW Bde with U Battery and Section of D A Col went up to MAMETZ Batteries are attached to Cavalry Brigade for Ammunition from this date. JEW	
27th Sept	Division moved to BUSSY les DOURS. Section of D.A. Col rejoined. Head Quarters in new area /over	

WAR DIARY

RHA Bde Hd Qrs, or 1st Ind Cav Division

INTELLIGENCE SUMMARY.

Army Form C. 2118.

Hour, Date, Place.	Summary of Events and Information.	Remarks and references to Appendices.
September 1916 28th ST PIERRE a GOUY	Division moved to new area. Bde Hd Qrs at PICQUINY R.H.A. Bde Hd Qrs and B a l of 16 to ST PIERRE a GOUY Batteries with Cavy Bdes. During the march Q Battery had one Gun Limber (Mark I) blown up by H.E. The supposed cause being a shell working loose from cartridge case & jolting up against the front of the Gun limber box. Four other Cartridges were burnt, the top of the Gun limber being blown off, and with the exception of the Off Wheeler receiving a severe head wound there were no other casualties. The No 1 and Wheel drivers showed great presence of mind by the way the gun was pulled and the fire extinguished. ↓	

Army Form C. 2118.

WAR DIARY
Gen. Qrs R.A. Brigade, 1st Can. Division

INTELLIGENCE SUMMARY.
(Erase heading not required.)

No 56

Hour. Date. Place.	Summary of Events and Information.	Remarks and references to Appendices.
September 1916		
29th COCQUEREL	Division marched to new area. Brit. H.Qrs. at AILLY le HAUT CLOCHER. Arty. Head Qrs. and D.A.C. at COCQUEREL. Few	
30th LIGESCOURT	Division marched to new area. Brit. Head Qrs at LIGESCOURT. R.A.Q. Head Qrs at Chateau just South of head E of Bois de St. SAULVE, South East of LIGESCOURT. D.A. Col at RAYE Sur AUTHIE. D.A.P. at LABROYE. Batteries with Infantry Brigades. Few	

30/9/1916

H. Westropp L.T.C.
for Brig. Gen R.A. 1st Can Div

SERIAL NO. 49

Confidential
War Diary
of

Headquarters 1st Indian F.H.A. Brigade.

FROM 1st October 1916 TO 30th November 1916
         31st October

Army Form C. 2118.

WAR DIARY

HEAD QUARTERS R.H.A Bde 1st INDIAN CAVY DIVN

INTELLIGENCE SUMMARY. No 57

(Erase heading not required.)

Place	Date 1916	Hour	Summary of Events and Information	Remarks and references to Appendices
LIGESCOURT	OCTOBER 2nd 14th		Bde Ammn Coln moved to ESTREE Le CRECY. Bde Ammln Park to LABROYE. /EuS Extract of 1st Ind Cavy Division Order No 299 d 14/10. The G.O.C in Chief has awarded the following decorations:- Military Medals 34731 Bomr E.B. CHILD U Bty. 47516 Sergt R.S. YATES. U Bty. 70481 Bdr R. MOBBS Q Bty. 24069 Bdr J. WILSON. A Bty. 34690 Dvr (Bdy) F. HARRIS. U Bty. 77296 Gnr P. PHILLIMORE Q Bty. 1073 Ammn Artfr S. Sgt W.C. WILLIS. (attached U Bty) Indian Order of Merit 2nd Class. — 1394 Indian Driver FUTEH JUNG U Bty /EuS Information that R.H.A Bde is to be prepared to move on 19th inst, and be attached to 1st Cavalry Division /EuS	
CHATEAU DRUCAS	19th		R.H.A Bde (less Ammunition Column which was left behind on account of Pink Eye) marched to new area. Head Quarters to CHATEAU DRUCAS. Batteries (marching independently) to NOEUX. Ammunition reports to 1st Cavy Division at FROHEN Le GRAND /EuS	
HAVERNAS	20th		Bde marched to HAVERNAS. Starting point WAVAN'S CHURCH 9 am. Arrived in Billets at 2.45pm. 1st Cavy Ammn Park and Gun Section of 1st IND. CAV Divn Park also in village having arrived on previous night /EuS	
LIGESCOURT	22nd	10.30 am 9.15 am	Bde returned to old Billets. Orders to march at 9.15 am received at 9.15 am - Bde did not move until 10.30 am. The return to old billets was in consequence of the Brigade having no Ammunition Column, the Army deciding to replace by 3rd Cavalry R.N.A Bde. Lt.Col CHARLTON. was retained as liaison between 5th Corps Heavy Artillery and one of the 5th Corps Divisions /EuS	

continued

Army Form C. 2118.

WAR DIARY
R.H.A. Eagle Head Qrs 1st Indn Cavy Division
INTELLIGENCE SUMMARY. No 58

(Erase heading not required.)

Place	Date	Hour	Summary of Events and Information	Remarks and references to Appendices
LIGESCOURT			OCTOBER 1916	
	30th		Extract from War office Gazette d/ 27-10-1916 Awarded Military Medal for bravery in the field. 63205 Bt. W. ROTHERHAM "A"/Bty. 49704 Gr STRUDWICK "A"/Bty. 52575 "B" EVERLEY "A"/Bty. 36493 Cpl R TAYLOR "Q" Bty. 49013 Dr ("B3") DURBIN "U" Bty. 16436 Gr WOOLGAR "U"/Bty. JEW Lt Col CHARLTON rejoined from attached St Corps JEW	
	31st		Orders received for march to winter billets on 2 Nov/16. JEW	
In the field 31/10/1916			J Eastrope LtRHA for Adjutant R.H.A.	

Army Form C. 2118.

WAR DIARY
R.H.A. Poole Head Qrs. (4th Cavalry Division)
INTELLIGENCE SUMMARY.
1st INDIAN CAV. DIV.   No. 59

NOVEMBER 1916

Place	Date	Hour	Summary of Events and Information	Remarks and references to Appendices
LIGESCOURT	2nd		Division moved into new billetting area	
ST VALLERY	4th		Div. H.Q. Qrs. ST VALLERY. R.H.A. Bde H.Q. Qrs. ST VALLERY. /FW/	
"			Lt. Col. C.E.C.G. CHARLTON, R.H.A. Commdg R.H.A. Bde left for 16th Division as Brig Genl. Sections of Div Ammn Column (less A Bty Section) are attached to their respective Batteries from this date. /FW/	
	9th		Div Ammn Coln changed billets from VALINES to FRESSENNEVILLE /FW/	
	16th		Lt. Col. H.C. ROCHFORT BOYD, D.S.O. joined the R.H.A. Bde /FW/	
	19th		Lt. C.F. CAMPBELL R.H.A reported from Base and rejoined U. Bty on 20th /FW/	
	19th		A. Battery proceeded by route march to join III Corps with Sections of D.A.C & D.A.P	
	19th		U. Battery proceeded by route march to 4th Army Arty. School at VAUX-in-AMIENOIS /FW/	
	23rd		Lt. W.K. HOLMES left U. Bty R.N.d. for 6th Division. /FW/	
	26th		1st Ind. and 2nd Ind. Cav. Divns changed to 4th and 5th Cav. Divns respectively. /FW/	
ST VALLERY	30th		Q Bty and its Section of D.A.C re armed with 13 pdrs & 13 Pdr Ammn Wagons in lieu of 18 pdrs. /FW/	

30-11-1916

J. Eldethorpe Lieut. R.H.A
for Adjutant R.H.A

SERIAL No. 49.

Confidential
War Diary
of

Headquarters 1st Indian R.H.A. Brigade.

FROM 1st December 1916. TO 31st December 1916.

Army Form C. 2118.

WAR DIARY
or
INTELLIGENCE SUMMARY.
(Erase heading not required.)

Instructions regarding War Diaries and Intelligence Summaries are contained in F. S. Regs., Part II. and the Staff Manual respectively. Title pages will be prepared in manuscript.

Place	Date	Hour	Summary of Events and Information	Remarks and references to Appendices
			CONFIDENTIAL.	
			WAR DIARY -- OF --	
			HEAD QUARTERS, 1st INDIAN R.H.A. BDE	
			FROM 1st DECEMBER 1916 TO 31st DECEMBER 1916.	
			(V O L U M E I.)	

Army Form C. 2118.

WAR DIARY
or Intelligence Summary.

R. H. A. Pde or Head Quarters, 1st Indian Cavalry Division

No. 60

(Erase heading not required.)

Place	Date	Hour	Summary of Events and Information	Remarks and references to Appendices
ST VALERY Sur SOMME.	DECEMBER 1916 11th		Information received that 13 pdrs would be issued to 'A' & 'U' Batteries in lieu of 18 pdrs. /JES/	
	16th		2/Lts COLES DARBY and FERDINANDO arrived at Divisional Ammunition Column and posted to 'A''U' and 'Q' Batteries respectively. /JES/ RFA	
	18th		Capt C. I. McKAY. A Battery R.H.A. posted to 2st Divisional Arty with a view to commanding a Battery R.F.A. /JES/	
	19th		Sergt RUSSELL Q Battery R.H.A. commissioned from 15 Dec 1916 and posted to 29th Division. /JES/	
	22nd		Lieut E.S.G. HOWARD. R.H.A.- (Adjutant) posted to 17.13y R.H.A. in relief of Capt C.I. McKAY /JEW/	
	26th		2Lieut F.E. WESTROPE R.F.A. appointed Adjutant in relief of Lt HOWARD. /JES/	
	29th		18 pdr Ammunition QBy (limbered) boxes and returned to No. 12 Ordnance Depot by Ammunition S.A.R. /JEW/	
	31-12-1916			

J E Westrope Lieut, R.H.A.
Adjutant, R.H.A. Pde

www.ingramcontent.com/pod-product-compliance
Lightning Source LLC
Chambersburg PA
CBHW081533160426
43191CB00011B/1752